Photograph by Frank Gerratana, Bridgeport Herald

CHARLES IVES

CHARLES IVES and His Music

CHARLES IVES

and His Music

---

by Henry Cowell and Sidney Cowell

NEW YORK

Oxford University Press · 1955

COPYRIGHT 1955 BY OXFORD UNIVERSITY PRESS, INC.

Library of Congress Catalogue Card Number: 54-10000

Printed in the United States of America

Preface

In so far as this is a personal record, Mr. and Mrs. Ives would much rather the book were never written.* But to the extent that it is a record of the progress toward acceptance of the music they so much believe in, and of the triumph of the Ideal, they are willing. The longer book originally planned would have been much more satisfactory in this respect, because it has been impossible to do justice here to all the various kinds of assistance that Mr. Ives's music has received, and which he would like to have acknowledged. Nor is the music's progress toward acceptance as documented as he would like, because this would entail lengthy quotations from reviews and letters to show increasing critical approval, for which there is not room here.

* When the authors first mentioned that a book about Ives had been proposed to them, Mrs. Ives hesitated. 'You know, I have never really liked seeing our name in print,' she said.

This progress can, however, be traced in its main outlines by means of the bibliography.*

It has seemed to the writers that a composer writes most usefully about another composer when he shows what goes on in the music and why, both from the craftsman's point of view and, if he can, from personal knowledge of his subject's creative intention. So the present book is history, not criticism. Its limitations, like its virtues if it has any, are inherent in its position as a first book about Ives, written during his lifetime by two friends, one of them a composer who has been associated with Ives and his music for twenty-six years.

Wherever possible, in the pages that follow, Ives speaks for himself. The quotations come not only from his book, the *Essays Before a Sonata* (1920), and from the other program notes, prologues, and epilogues that he has had printed with his music, but also from a fragmentary autobiographical manuscript written mostly between 1931 and 1937 as nearly as we can determine, parts of which have been several times corrected, added to, or rewritten, parts of which are incomplete. This manuscript was given by Mr. Ives to the writers about 1949, for use in this book.

In spite of the generosity with which Mr. and Mrs. Ives have permitted the invasion of their privacy with respect to family records, papers, and photographs, this is in no sense an authorized biography. Mr. and Mrs. Ives have not been shown the manuscript, nor have they asked to see it. The authors alone must take responsibility for many interpretations and syntheses made for the sake of that 'curious definiteness of man' which Mr. Ives has more than once deplored.

The trail of first performances is confused to the point where we can find no such claim, however honestly made (and even sometimes innocently confirmed by the composer), that does not have to be qualified. Either somebody else played the work

* The bibliography is not exhaustive; it includes articles and a few reviews selected because they were early, or especially inclusive, or especially illuminating, or because they came at a significant moment in the music's history.

earlier somewhere else; or a part of it had already been played in New York; or it appeared on some program in a different version or under a different title. Having given up the idea that even modest accuracy in this respect is possible, we have not tried to list first performances at all. A footnote for the *Concord Sonata* illustrates the problems. We should like to suggest a new notation for programs: 'This work has been deservedly played (or sung) many times before.'

Adequate recognition of the wholly generous help we have had would fill pages. Our special appreciation goes to Lucille Fletcher, who turned over for our use an unpublished article with information about Charles Ives's boyhood that had been obtained in an interview with Moss Ives only a week before he died. John Becker, Mrs. Henry Bellamann, Wallingford Riegger, E. Robert Schmitz, and Nicolas Slonimsky have loaned personal letters from Ives or letters written for him by his wife and daughter. Other help came from Julian Myrick and Mrs. Bellamann; and Nicolas Slonimsky not only contributed stacks of invaluable early programs, but took time to check over the manuscript with his experienced eye, as did Jack Taylor in the role of 'general reader.' Elizabeth Ames, George Avakian, Leonard Bernstein, B. H. Bronson, Elliott Carter, Robert K. Clark, Aaron Copland, Richard Donovan, Lehman Engel, John Tasker Howard, John Jennings, John Kirkpatrick, Julius Mattfeld, Osea Noss, Mrs. Vincent Persichetti, Quincy Porter, Frank Wigglesworth, and Peter Yates have all made helpful replies to our appeals for information, some of them more than once, and like the resourceful music librarians at the Library of Congress, the New York Public Library at 42nd Street, the University of California at Berkeley, and the American Music Center in New York, they are all remembered gratefully. Edith Ives Tyler has been consistently helpful, and we are most grateful to Mr. and Mrs. Ives for their patience with an enterprise that has surely, from their point of view, been very trying.

Gorham Munson and Henry James originally proposed the book to us in 1947, and we hope they will like the way it has turned out. Carroll Bowen and Leona Capeless as editors, and

Alf Evers as a Catskill Mountains neighbor of skill and experience, have been generous with the finest possible professional help over stiles, past technical traps, and through mazes and thickets, as Nathan Broder was earlier. And it is not too much to say that without the spirit of good will and the stenographic skill of Gene Scherpenberg at Shady, New York, and Ilse Schlanger in Berkeley, California, the book would still be unfinished.

We have declined the editor's very reasonable suggestion that each author should sign one part of the book. We have both worked on it at intervals for seven years, and it would be impossible now to unravel our individual contributions to it. In general SRC is responsible for the biographical section and HC for the section on the music, but there has been endless cross-fertilization. At the rare points where it matters, it should be evident which author is speaking.

The quotations that stand at the beginning of each chapter come either from Ives's own writings in the postscript to the *114 Songs* and in the *Essays Before a Sonata,* or else from Emerson's *Essays* and Thoreau's *Walden* as quoted by Ives. 'A Terribly Hard Taste of Music' was the headline for the first review of the *Concord Sonata.* 'A kind of furious calm' is a comment by Ives on Emerson.

Henry Cowell
Sidney Robertson Cowell

Shady, New York
15 May 1954

•   •   •

Charles Ives died in New York on 19 May 1954, in his eightieth year. As he himself often pointed out, 'There is always something more to be said,' and his death naturally marks the beginning of a new phase in the life of his music. The present study, however, was made during his lifetime and it necessarily retains that point of view.

Contents

Part One

——————

LIFE

'I desire to speak somewhere without bounds like a man in a waking moment to men in their waking moments . . . for I am convinced that I cannot exaggerate enough even to lay a foundation for a true expression . . .'

—HENRY DAVID THOREAU

Quoted by Ives in *Essays Before a Sonata*

I

Time and Place

———

Nobody today writes just like Charles Ives because no one lives in the same musical and philosophical world he did. He has taught no pupils, he has founded no 'school.' At the same time, nobody today seems to be able to think up any kind of musical behavior that cannot be found, sometimes in embryo, sometimes fully worked out, in the music of Ives. His mature creative life covered little more than twenty years, yet his manuscripts contain a whole new world of music, prophetically suggesting or developing aspects of music whose 'discovery' was to make other men famous for years to come.

3

Ives can, in fact, be shown to be one of the four great creative figures in music of the first half of the twentieth century. The others are Schoenberg, Stravinsky, and Bartók. No composer has escaped the influences of the first two — influences that seem now fairly fully assimilated. Bartók and Ives, on the other hand, stand for something new whose power is only beginning to be felt, and which undoubtedly has many years to run. Both men went back deliberately into unsophisticated music to explore and then carry forward aspects of musical behavior that had gone unnoticed or had been abandoned by the eighteenth- and nineteenth-century composers who established the symphonic music of the Western world. Bartók's source was the folk music of Central Europe and the Near East. Ives's music had its roots in the church, stage, parlor, and dance music of a small American town — the popular music of his time, in short.

Charles Ives was born in 1874 in Danbury, Connecticut, not far from the place where his forebears settled soon after the landing of the Pilgrims. He has been identified with this part of New England all his life, although he was for many years in business in New York. His father was a Civil War band leader and music teacher in Danbury; his mother was one of the soloists in a Danbury church choir.

There were composers in New England before Charles Ives, but none who questioned the value of European culture for America or who appreciated the music around him at home. If Charles Ives has been called the father of American music by American composers themselves, this is not so much because he has sired descendants who imitate his music,* but because he spoke out so strongly his determina-

* Ives's music has for so long been more written about than performed that it could not be expected to have much influence on the developing styles of American music. But around 1950 a number of

4

tion to discover what it meant to be a musician as the twentieth century began in America. He was the first composer in the United States to commit himself unreservedly to the vernacular for the grammar of a new symphonic speech. It was his example that lent a decisive strength to younger men who hoped to speak for themselves and for their own world. Every American writing music today is the more independently and confidently himself because of the courage with which Ives obeyed Thoreau's injunction:

> *Direct your eye right inward . . . and so be*
> *Expert in home-cosmography.*

To experiment and to explore has never been revolutionary for an American; he is unaffectedly at home in the unregulated and the untried. In a vast new country experience is direct, intense and various, and so grass-roots creative activity in the United States has been marked by an exuberance and a diversity that are shocking to sensibilities developed in older cultures whose essence is refinement and selectivity. In all the arts Americans quite naturally bring together elements that elsewhere appear as irreconcilable canons of radically opposed schools of thought.

---

scores for films or Broadway plays whose musical character owed something to the actual music of Ives began to be heard by large audiences: Alex North's music for *Death of a Salesman*, for one; Bernard Herrmann's score for the film *Anna and the King of Siam*, for another; and Jerome Moross' ballet *The Last Judgment*. It now seems that the question as to what American music would have become had the actual music of Ives been widely played is having a belated answer. Interestingly enough, this musical influence did not appear first in symphonic music for concert, but in music that addresses the same audiences as the theater orchestras that appealed to Ives as a young man around 1900. In 1953 the tapesichord music of Otto Luening and Vladimir Ussachevsky, and the multi-directional symphonic music written by Henry Brant for groups under several conductors, began to invade formal concert halls with the development of ideas that stem from Ives.

Inherited traditions, with all their subtleties, are necessarily pushed aside when the time comes to reinvigorate art with a transfusion from more immediate experience.

This is not because Americans are determined on iconoclasm or eccentricity. They are just anxious to be themselves, to establish their relation to life and art straight from within. Such an attitude is far from being the expression of a personal romanticism. It is rather a spiritual concept which stems from the gospel preached by the Transcendentalists at Concord, who believed that man, nature, and God are one, and that truth and integrity are attainable by man only to the degree that he perceives his own identity with the creative forces of the universe, on which alone he may depend. This is a philosophy of the Ideal whose emphasis is on what could be, on the intuitively sensed possibility that is illimitable, rather than on what has been or what other people are.

Charles Ives was still a boy when, early on a Memorial Day morning, a moment of revelation of 'an exultant something gleaming with the possibilities of this life, an assurance that nothing is impossible,' gave him a sense of the Universal lying behind the appearances of nature and all material things, and marked him for its search. Much later he was to write: 'There comes from Concord an offer to every man — the choice between repose and truth.' Ives chose truth, and it seemed natural to him, as it had to another Yankee named Thoreau, to search for that truth in his own vision of the life — and the sounds — around him. So he pondered the relations of things, testing out music by life and life by music, and building abstract musical structures like concrete events. This makes his particular kind of program music, in which the flow of musical relationships derives from the patterns of activity he saw around him. The music therefore records not a *thing* that happens but the *way* things happen. Because events don't move by singly, but carry memories and forecasts with them, colliding and conflicting with other events too, Ives's music moves in many directions at once and is built on many levels, in the way that experience comes to the mind.

The techniques that Ives discovered or explored are still fresh and alive in music today, and so it is easy to forget that when he was a boy he listened to the philosophical disquisitions of Civil War veterans, and that his productive period as a composer came to a close with the First World War. He has always been a highly articulate man, and he found compatible bedrock for his thinking and writing about music in the New England Transcendentalists, whose attitude toward life placed so indelible an imprint on the developing American character after the middle of the nineteenth century. In his profoundly moral New England environment, the counsel of the Concord philosophers was examined right along with the Bible and applied literally to every human concern. For his own creed Ives drew on Emerson, and on the uncomfortable Thoreau for courage; it is not too much to say that all his life he has been closer to these two than to any living man. 'Be strong to live!' Emerson had exclaimed to a group of young Americans, 'Have confidence in the unsearched might of man . . . We have listened too long to the courtly muses of Europe . . . We will walk on our own feet, we will work with our own hands, we will speak our own minds . . . Give me insight into today and you may have the antique and future worlds.'

The music that belongs to any organic culture has always had to wait longer than the other arts to find its characteristic and integrated expression. So the music most naturally in accord with the eager, independent, and vehemently idealistic New England temper did not emerge until the turn of the century when, between 1896 and 1916 for the most part, Charles Edward Ives set his sweeping and emphatic notes on paper. By that time Emerson's thinking had been shaping American minds for more than sixty years, without affecting the practice of music at all.

Until after the First World War, American composers of symphonic music were almost without exception trained in Europe by Europeans, and they absorbed the esthetics of the older civilization along with its techniques. At the time that Ives struck out for himself, Central Europe had been the center of the musical culture of the Western world for 250 years, and a composer from raw America who presented himself there as a student would never dream, nor would he have been allowed, to question the canons of musical composition that were given him as absolute law. From Lowell Mason in the first half of the nineteenth century to Paine, Parker, Chadwick, and Foote, Americans naïvely agreed with their teachers that what a composer wrote was right or wrong depending on how exactly it could be made to resemble what was done in Europe, and they could not wait to get home to 'improve musical standards in America.' Transplanted to the United States, the rules of harmony and composition took on a doctrinaire authority that was the more dogmatic for being second hand. Edward MacDowell felt something unnatural about this, but he was never able to depart from his well-schooled European handling of American programmatic or pictorial ideas.

This was a period when new musical materials were approached with extreme timidity when they were used at all. Moreover, they had to be organized so that they would connect carefully with what had gone before, for it seemed desirable not to shock the ears of cultivated people nor the much vaunted 'canons of good taste.' No one was ready to admit that good taste in the old urban societies of Europe and in the dynamic abundant immensity of America could hardly be the same thing.

Yet a system of esthetics is born after the event, derived by students from the new worlds made by artists. Ives stayed at home to develop musical relationships and types of musical behavior that matched his thematic starting points and that were in accord with what he heard in his own rural American sound world. Native speech, he thought with Emerson, could only develop out of the 'common sense' — a sense, that is, of the common, the ordinary, the every-day.

Emerson had warned the young apostles of distinction at Harvard: 'Perception of the worth of the vulgar is fruitful in discoveries,' and Ives intended to see that these discoveries were made. He has never given a good Continental damn whether 'nice' people think the sounds in his music are 'pretty' or 'logical' or 'in good taste.' But he made sure that the sounds had meaning in the expression of his feeling and philosophy. His music is marked by an unprecedented drive and breadth and inclusiveness, an overwhelming sense of the fullness of life. Like Whitman, Ives passionately, even vociferously, asserted the right of the American artist to be himself and therefore different from any European, and both men drew on the same flooding prose rhythms to express what they felt in the world. They were both constrained, as well, to lifelong insistence that a preoccupation with art and a profound feeling for the common man have nothing about them that is incompatible with a rugged masculinity and all the heroic pioneer virtues.

While Ives's music is not always dissonant, any more than men always fight, still the hearers he hopes for are the kind who take delight in strong sound and who respond, with vigor equal to his own, to big bold ideas. The mere mention of certain composers sets Ives to humming sardonically under his breath, to the theme of Haydn's *Surprise Symphony*: 'Pret-ty lit-tle sug-ar plum sounds . . .' That man's music, as far as Ives is concerned, is utterly damned: Easy music for the sissies, for the lilypad ears of Rollo! * Ives, on the other hand, concludes a piano sketch with the note: 'To strengthen and give more muscle to the ear, brain, heart, limbs and FEAT! Atta boy!' Elsewhere he admonishes himself marginally: 'Keep up our fight! — ART! — hard at it — don't quit because the ladybirds † don't like it!'

In less aggressive but no less earnest mood, Ives wrote: 'But we would rather believe . . . that the time is coming, but not in our lifetime, when music will develop possibilities inconceivable now — a language, so transcendent, that its heights and depths will be common to all mankind.'

In the course of one of Ives's brief songs for voice and piano there is the notation: 'These four measures sound better sung with string quartet if one is available.' Four string players are not usually on hand at a song recital to play just the four measures that sound better with strings than they do with piano, but of course from the composer's point of view they should be. Ives exclaims: 'Why can't a musical thought be presented as it is born? That music must be heard is not essential — what it *sounds* like may not be what it *is*.' Once a singer wrote to say regretfully that she liked a certain song but found it really impossible

* An imaginary gentleman named Rollo is a familiar of the Ives household — one of those white-livered weaklings who cannot stand up and receive the full force of a dissonance like a man.

† Ladybirds are Rollos en masse who sit in boxes. They sometimes conduct orchestras, write reviews, or hold professorships in colleges, and there have been a number of them on the concert stage.

to sing. Ives replied that probably the song was quite unsingable and she should not let it worry her. He just felt the song demanded to be written that way, and that it should be allowed a life of its own, even if no human being happened to be so constructed as to be able to sing it. Ives's *Universe Symphony* is the ultimate expression of this unfettered imagination, carried quite beyond all human limitations.

Behind Charles Ives there was another powerfully imaginative and experimental mind, the mind of his father, George Ives. The germ of every new type of musical behavior that Charles Ives developed or organized can be found in the suggestions and experiments of his father, the busy bandmaster of Danbury, Connecticut. At the same time, it was due to his father's insistence that Charles Ives as a boy was trained in all the conventional ways of treating music too.

George Ives was a lively jack-of-all-musical-trades in his community: he played the piano for dances, the organ for church, taught almost any musical instrument, led bands, choirs, and chamber music groups, and made arrangements. But he was not a composer. He liked, however, to try out new sound relationships with the material at his command — his band, his students, his family and friends. He was intrigued by musical happenstance, welcoming and examining the peculiarities of accidental rhythmic and tonal collision, as when two children played finger exercises in two different keys in adjacent houses, or when a passer-by whistled down the street while his wife, Mary Ives, sang a hymn in the kitchen — all audible to George Ives, standing between them, and interesting. Some such collisions he later arranged himself, as will be seen. They remained in his son's mind as possible patterns for broader musical development, and later on this is what he gave them. The parallels in thinking between the two men are profound and surprising. His father's is the influence Charles Ives most proudly acknowledges, and it is not too much to say that the son has written his father's music for him.

In spite of its reputation most of Ives's music is perfectly possible, but it *is* difficult. Every great creative figure in music has stretched the unwilling ears and minds of performers toward a new concept of the meaningful, the beautiful, and the practical. Unlike a poet or a painter, a composer is dependent on his interpreters; there is always another and very differently oriented musical mind standing between him and his audience. Concert performers normally believe the music of greatest meaning to lie somewhere behind them. As a great creative mind is by definition prophetic, only rarely will he find a great performer able to follow him sympathetically. This has always been true even when a composer and his interpreters were brought up in the same tradition. If Charles Ives has had to wait longer than anyone else for his music to be heard, it is because conductors and performers had a double discovery to make — a new world had to become real to them before they could believe in its music.

Ives never heard a major orchestra work played for an audience and as he wrote it until long after he had to stop composing, and this is perhaps one reason why he continued to plow virgin soil and to open up one new area after another to the imagination. Most of his symphonic works were tried over in part by a small theater orchestra, but a great many important instruments were missing, of course, and no real attempt was made to perform any of his major orchestra works as a whole until 1931 or so. This certainly bothered him less than it would most people, for ten years after he had allowed the *Concord Sonata* (No. 2 for piano) to be crystallized in print, he wrote:

> . . . the Emerson movement . . . This is as far as I know the only piece which every time I play it or turn to it seems unfinished . . . It is a peculiar experience and I must admit a stimulating and agreeable one that I have had with this Emerson music. It may have something to do with the feeling I have about Emerson, for every time I read him, I seem to get a new angle of thought and feeling and experience from him. Some of the four transcriptions as I play them today, especially in the first and third, are changed considerably from those in the photostat, and again I find that I do not play or feel like playing this music even now in the same way each time.
>
> Some of the passages now played have not been written out, and I do not know as I ever shall write them out as it may take away the daily pleasure of playing this music and seeing it grow and feeling that it is not finished and the hope that it never will be — I may always have the pleasure of not finishing it.

Both Ives's background and his temperament combined to cast him in the role of explorer and pioneer; his mind was never on the distillation of experience that makes for a stylized brevity and unity of utterance. He was convinced that fertility of idea and the release of fresh energy were more important to the music of his day than the painstaking refinement of a tradition that seemed threadbare to him when it was not irrelevant. Today, more than thirty years after he last undertook a new work, most of the things that were considered both outrageous and impossible when he first set them down are played with conviction and found beautiful. Indeed, no American hears the *Concord Sonata,*

The Housatonic at Stockbridge, the *Harvest Home Chorales, In the Inn,* or *The Unanswered Question* without a shock of recognition. Ives is the composer Emerson was expecting when he wrote: 'He finds that he is the complement of his hearers; that they drink his words because he fulfills for them their own nature . . . The better part of every man feels: This is my music, this is myself.' So in spite of long frustration, illness, and isolation, the life of Ives is a triumphant one.

I I

George Ives and His Son Charlie

―――――――

'A FOUNDATION FOR A TRUE EXPRESSION'

'That's a good band,' President Lincoln remarked. 'It's the best band in the Army, they tell me,' General Grant replied. 'But you couldn't prove it by me. I know only two tunes: one of them is Yankee Doodle, and the other isn't.' So ran a conversation during the siege of Richmond, according to one of Grant's officers. The band under discussion was the Brigade Band of the First Connecticut Heavy Artillery. Its leader was George E. Ives, then just seventeen years old.

When the war was over George Ives went back to Danbury, bringing with him a small colored boy whose mother had done the washing for the band and whom George Ives was teaching to read and write both music and English. In accordance with the strong Abolitionist convictions of the Ives family, the boy was taken in and sent to school in Danbury. He later became a famous teacher, one of the strong influences at Hampton; his name was Anderson Brooks.

No New England village of the period could hold its own among neighboring rivals without the aggregation of musicians known as a Cornet Band. The instrumentation was dictated by the taste of the players and the availability of instruments, and it varied from year to year and from town to town, so that violins, violas, and flutes were not unusual. George Ives undertook to produce such a group at Danbury, rounding up willing but untrained candidates and teaching them the instrument of their choice. In a surprisingly short time the Danbury Band was distinguishing itself at holiday parades and ball games, not only at home but in near-by towns. Its accomplishments were much admired; its leader, after all, had had sound conventional training in music theory from a number of teachers, some of them as far away as New York City.

Because music teaching in this country was suffering under a rigid, second-hand German academicism, the average American's experience of art music during most of the nineteenth century was so overwhelmingly dull, stiff, and meaningless that only 'popular' music, — stage, dance, and folk music — had any vitality. A real interest in music and any care for excellence in it was considered only fit for marriageable girls to offer as a drawing-room accomplishment; musical talent in a boy was deprecated and derided.

George Ives, however, was entirely independent in this as in other ways. He never doubted the human significance of the country church and dance music that was such a living part of American life; he found it as moving as

Beethoven, whose music he also loved. He never stopped studying and exploring on his own account: conventional music theory he conceived as merely a point of departure for his own thinking. This was, of course, the prevalent New England attitude toward all European systems of thought.

The only recorded evidence of a musical streak in the Ives family before George Ives is the activity of a distant connection, Elam Ives of Hartford. He was the compiler and editor of a number of books of the type used in the New England singing schools, notably *American Psalmody* (Hartford, 1829), the *Musical Spelling Book* (New York, 1846), and, collaborating with Lowell Mason in an attempt to elevate musical taste in children by the use of German folk tunes with English words, the *Juvenile Lyre* (Boston, 1835). The sections of these books dealing with the rudiments of music and the 'inductive method of instruction in musical elocution' are unusually complete and sophisticated for the time. These books seem not to have been known to either George Ives or his son.

On 1 January 1874, George Ives married Mary Parmelee, who was the daughter of the leading church soloist of the village. Her father was a Yankee farmer whose great ambition was to invent perpetual motion and apply it to various of the world's problems.

Charles Edward Ives was born to George and Mary Parmelee Ives on 20 October 1874, in Danbury. His mother is remembered as a good neighbor and a staunch friend, a conscientious New England housewife forever trying to keep rubbers on her husband and sons, and to inveigle them into starched collars. Mr. Ives and Charlie, whose interest in music she approved without entirely sharing, seem always to have been too preoccupied to co-operate wholly with her concern for a respectable appearance. Her younger son, Moss, was more like his mother.

The Ives family had been established in Connecticut by Captain William Ives, who came from Dorchester in England on the *Truelove* and landed in Boston in 1635. He was one of the original party to settle Quinnipiak in Connecticut (now a part of New Haven) in 1638; his signature is on the Quinnipiak Civil Compact of 1639. His descendants for the most part seem to have remained uninterruptedly in Connecticut during the nine successive generations — farmers, parsons, bankers, and lawyers, respected as solid citizens. At least one member of the family did venture abroad, however, for there is a family record of an ancestor who in the eighteenth century sold his farm in New York City, at what is now Beekman Street and the East River, because the place was getting too fancy and crowded for his taste. Charles Ives lives only a few miles away from his birthplace today.

One of young Charlie's earliest memories is of his father standing in the back garden at Danbury, without hat or coat in a heavy thunderstorm, and listening in exasperation to the ringing of the church bell next door. Try as he might he couldn't find the exact combination on the piano to reproduce it, and he ran out into the storm to listen and then back to the keyboard, over and over again. It may be that he finally concluded, rightly, that the tones in the bell were not in the piano, for not long afterward he began to build a machine that would play the tones 'in the cracks between the piano keys.'

George Ives had absolute pitch, but such a gift did not conform to his ideas about things and he found it more upsetting than anything else. 'Everything in life is relative,' he used to say. 'Nothing but fools and taxes are absolute.'

Once when a friend who was 'a thorough musician' (he had graduated from the New England Conservatory of Music in Boston) showed surprise at the senior Ives's love of banging out dissonances at the piano, and asked how with his sensitive ear he could possibly stand it, Ives answered drily: '*I* may have absolute pitch, but thank God, that piano hasn't.'

The idea of dividing the octave to produce intervals smaller than the half-tone had of course occurred to more than one exploring musical mind: in the Moscow Conservatory of Music there is a piano built to play quarter tones which is dated 1864. At the Philadelphia Exposition of 1875, Karl Rudolph Koenig demonstrated a tonometric apparatus dividing four octaves into 670 parts. It is not certain that George Ives knew of this experiment, but one of Helmholtz's books was in the family library, and the elder Ives certainly devoted much time and thought, over a period of many years, to the splitting of what was by most people considered to be the irreducible musical atom, the half-tone.

The instrument that he built seems not to have worked out too well. It consisted of twenty-four violin strings stretched across a clothes-press; they were let down with weights. He found it simpler to tune glasses to produce quarter-tones and other very small intervals; and the slide cornet was helpful too. Once he was able to sound the actual intervals, he drew on his family and friends for assistance in discovering how adaptable they were to human musical use.

In an article for *Pro Musica Quarterly,* Charles Ives wrote in 1925:

> My father had a weakness for quarter-tones — in fact he didn't stop even with them. He rigged up a contrivance to stretch 24 or more violin strings and tuned

them up to suit the dictates of his own curiosity. He would pick out quarter-tone tunes and try to get the family to sing them. But I remember he gave that up, except as a means of punishment, though we got to like some of the tunes which kept to the usual scale and had quarter-tone notes thrown in. After working for some time he became sure that some quarter-tone chords must be learned before quarter-tone melodies would make much sense and become natural to the ear and so for the voice.

He started to apply a system of bows to be released by weights which would sustain the chords — but in this process he was suppressed by the family and a few of the neighbors. A little later on he did some experimenting with glasses and bells and got some sounds as beautiful sometimes as they were funny — a complex that only children are old enough to appreciate.

But I remember distinctly one impression (and this was about 35 years ago). After getting used to hearing a piano piece when the upper melody, runs, etc., were filled out with quarter-tone notes (as a kind of ornamentation), when the piece was played on the piano alone there was a very keen sense of dissatisfaction — of something wanted but missing.

His son recalls other experiments: he tuned a piano in actual partials, to match the sounds of the overtone series, and he devised and tried out, again with tuned glasses, some new scales without octaves. He was interested in echoes and played his instruments one at a time over Danbury Pond, which amplified the echo that came back to him. He made endless attempts to imitate the sound of the echo itself, which he recognized as being different in quality — in tone color as well as in volume — from the initial tone.

On certain national holidays, such as Washington's Birthday or the Fourth of July, it was usual for several bands from the country near by to join under George Ives's leadership in Danbury, and he would sometimes try breaking them up into sections that were stationed about, one perhaps up in the church steeple, another on the roof of the Danbury News Building on Main Street, and a third on the village green. Each section would play, in turn, a variation on *Greenland's Icy Mountains* or *Jerusalem the Golden* specially composed for it.

Another device he enjoyed working out was what he called the humanophone, an arrangement of singers in which each person sang a different tone of the scale, and that one alone, sounding his tone only when the tune called for that particular note. Charles Ives occasionally used this idea in songs with difficult melodic leaps, suggesting that the successive tones of the melody be sung by different voices. He has also applied the idea of separating groups of players in some of his orchestral music. In the Fourth Symphony, for example, the matter of relative intensities requires, to Ives's mind, that members of the various instrumental sections be placed on different parts of the stage, and even in the auditorium, to control the distance the sound travels from the sounding body to the listening ear. This is for the sake of variety in intensity, since the effect of tones played loudly at a distance is very different from the same tones played softly close at hand.

Father had a kind of natural interest in sounds of every kind, known or unknown, 'measured as such' or not, and this led him into situations that made some of the townspeople call him a crank whenever he appeared in public with some of his contraptions . . . (which was not often) . . . This interest in this side of music took all his extra time. He did but little composing — a few things or arrangements for bands.

In fact, he had little interest in composition for himself, and it is too bad, for it would have shown these interests, and it would have been in some keepable form. He did not write textbooks, and did not write many letters; he left little behind except his memories in others.

Such a free-ranging mind, active in the entire world of sound, created fine growing conditions for his son Charlie. Moreover, George Ives appreciated the flavor of the rural music around him and encouraged the boy to find the fun and beauty in it. Charles Ives still admires his father more than any musician he has ever known.

Father had a gift for playing. He would take a familiar piece and play it to make it mean more than something just usual. The things he played then were mostly the things that most bands play, but he put something in them that most band leaders did not.

Charlie Ives hung around his father's band rehearsals from the time he could walk. Almost everyone in the community was an active participant in music in one way or another, either at church meeting or dances or in the band or during musical evenings at home. The atmosphere was full of animation and pleasure in sound, and the music had a beauty both vehement and crude. Ives's environment, compared with the professional training offered by the best conservatories in Europe, was in many ways provincial and limited, but it had an immense vitality. Its source was quite different from that of the music current in the sophisticated concert world, since it came largely from the music most familiar and beloved by the greatest number of Americans: that is, from the popular music of the time.

In Ives's boyhood, this music took many forms. He heard

more than one kind of highly expert fiddling for dances, played as a matter of course with a clean technical skill and a hard-driving rhythm rarely matched on the concert stage. He heard several kinds of hymn singing: the old, slow, melodically decorated psalm singing that goes back to Puritan times, the strenuous revival hymns of the outdoor camp meetings, and the romantic four-part hymns of the more elegant village churches. He knew all the popular songs composed by a friend of his father's named Stephen Foster, and their relatives the minstrel tunes, and he was acquainted with the sentimental parlor music, the tear-jerking ballads, and ripply arpeggios that young ladies liked to perform. He went to country fairs, and, somewhat later, to small theaters and minstrel shows, where he enjoyed the random instrumental combinations which were to appear so often in his own music.

As far back as he can remember a great deal of chamber music was played by his father and his friends — sonatas, trios, and quartets — chosen from the sturdier sorts by Handel, Bach, and Beethoven. They were performed with gusto by unexpected combinations of brass, woodwinds, strings, piano or organ — combinations that would have amused, without greatly surprising, the composers. Haydn and Mozart were never popular with either George or Charles Ives; they were considered too sweet, too pretty, too easy on the ears.

At the outdoor camp-meeting services in Redding all the farmers, their families, field hands and friends for miles around would come afoot or in their farm wagons. I remember how the great waves of sound used to come through the trees when things like *Beulah Land, Woodworth, Nearer My God to Thee, The Shining Shore, Nettleton, In the Sweet Bye-and-Bye,* and the like, were sung by thousands of 'let-out' souls. The music notes and words on paper are about as much like what they were at those moments as the monogram on a man's necktie may be like his face. Father, who led the singing, sometimes with his cornet or his voice, sometimes with both voice and arms, and sometimes in the quieter hymns with a violin or French horn, would always encourage the people to sing their own way. Most of them knew the words and music (their version) by heart and sang it that way. If they threw the poet or composer around a bit, so much the better for the poetry and the music. There was power and exaltation in these great conclaves of sound from humanity.

Once when Father was asked: 'How can you stand it to hear old John Bell (who was the best stonemason in town) bellow off-key the way he does at camp-meetings?' his answer was: 'Old John is a supreme musician. Look into his face and hear the music of the ages. Don't pay too much attention to the sounds. If you do, you may miss the music. You won't get a heroic ride to Heaven on pretty little sounds!'

Young Charles was about eight years old when his father found him at the piano in the music room of the old family house on Danbury's Main Street, perched high on a green velvet stool and banging away earnestly all by himself in an attempt to play not a melody but the rhythms he had heard on the drums in the Danbury Band. 'It's all right to do that, Charlie,' said his father, voicing a principle the boy was to hear expressed a thousand times during his later studies under his father's guidance. 'It's all right to do that, *if* you know what you're doing.'

Soon thereafter Mr. Ives marched the boy down to the village barber shop and turned him over to the barber, an old German bandsman named Slier, who played the drum in Ives's Danbury Civil War Band. Old Mr. Slier gave the youngster an empty tub and a couple of drumsticks, and settled him on a stool just under the shelf that held the customers' shaving mugs. There, between shaves and haircuts, he taught Charlie the double roll and all the other things a good drummer was expected to know. By the time he was twelve, Charlie was confidently playing the snare drum in his father's band.

In practising the drum parts on the piano alone (without the other players), I remember getting tired of using the tonic and dominant and subdominant triads, with doh and sol in the bass. So I got to trying sets of notes to 'take off' the drums — for the snare drum, right-hand notes usually closer together, and for the bass drum, left-hand notes and wider intervals. They had little to do with the harmony of the piece, and were used only as sound combinations and as such.
For the explosive notes or heavy accents in either drum, the fist or flat of the hand was sometimes used, usually longer groups with the right hand than with the left hand . . . Triads were quite out of place (chords without bites to them) and any combination that suggested a fixed tonality was not needed. Sometimes when practising with others or the small orchestra, I would play the drum parts on the piano, and I noticed that it did not seem to bother the other players, if I would keep away from triads or anything else that suggested a key. A popular chord in the right hand was doh-sharp, me, sol, doh-natural. Sometimes a rah-sharp on top; and one with 2 white notes with thumb, but having the little fingers run into a 7th or an 8ve and a semi-tone over the lower thumb note. The left hand would often

25

take 2 black notes on top with the thumb and run down the rest on white or measured intervals.

What started as boy play and in fun, gradually worked into something that had a serious side to it which opened up possibilities, sometimes valuable ones, as the ears got used to and acquainted with these many various dissonant sound combinations . . . And on going back to the usual consonant triads, something strong seemed more or less missing.

The boy's music was not confined to the drum, however, for Mr. Ives taught his son piano, violin, cornet, sight-reading, and harmony, as well as counterpoint — all on the strictest academic principles. Experiment, he told his son, could come later. He must first learn the rudiments thoroughly, so that when the time came to try out ideas of his own, his experiments would have some sense to them.

However, unlike most of his contemporaries, Charlie was never led to believe that the rules covered all of music. Although he was not at first encouraged to experiment much himself, he was a fascinated spectator and assistant in his father's explorations of acoustics, natural sounds, new instrumental sounds, and so on. Much early practical experience with instruments in each category, strings, wood-winds, brass, and percussion, gave him a knowledge of instruments and their possibilities far beyond that possessed by most aspiring composers at that time. Charlie was a fluent arranger of music for his father's various small ensemble combinations by the time he was thirteen years old. He was eleven when he first began to study the organ; he was then already fairly proficient at the piano. Two years later he was holding down a regular job as organist of the West Street Congregational Church in Danbury, which required him to play two services on Sunday. In addition he gave frequent recitals.

Several years earlier he had begun to compose. The first piece he wrote was a dirge for Chin-Chin, the family cat. This led to a series of commissions from friends for funeral music for assorted pets, and later Charlie even wrote a passacaglia based on the *Dead March* from *Saul* at the death of the family dog. These pieces were for various instruments, depending upon available performers. At thirteen he composed a band piece, *Holiday Quick Step*. This was the first of Charles Ives's compositions to win comment in the public press; it was approved and the young composer applauded. When a little later the piece was performed by the band for the Decoration Day parade, Charlie was too overcome to appear in his usual place at the snare drum. Instead, when the band came marching down Main Street past the Ives house playing Charlie's piece full tilt, the boy was discovered nervously playing handball against the barn door, with his back to the parade.

A year later, at fourteen, he was hired for a bigger job as organist at the First Baptist Church, an event remarked on by the *Danbury News,* 20 October 1888: 'Charles Ives presided at the organ at the Baptist Church yesterday. He is the youngest organist in the State.' By this time he was writing music for the organ and composing songs and instrumental pieces. But he dreaded being called a 'piano player' by other boys his age. It was all right to be called a ball player, however. When people fussed over his music and asked what he played, he liked to reply gruffly: 'Shortstop!' On 12 June 1890, one of his organ recitals began with the Overture to *William Tell,* and continued with *Home, Sweet Home* and Lemmens's *March Pontificale* in D, both arranged by Dudley Buck, a Bach toccata, and Mendelssohn's F-minor Organ Sonata.

Charlie attended the Danbury Academy, then the Danbury High School, and went on to the Hopkins Preparatory School in New Haven, to get ready to enter Yale. He liked sports and was good at them. He was captain, in turn, of the football teams at the Danbury Academy and the Danbury High School, and while he was at Hopkins he pitched on the baseball team that beat the Yale freshmen in a ten-inning game. Nothing so fine had happened at Hopkins since Walter Camp's days as a player there, and in celebration Rector Fox gave the school a 'holiday hour.' Meanwhile, the boy continued to play the organ and above all to compose. About the first 'large and serious' pieces that he can now recall were a communion service, performed at St. James's Church in Danbury in 1889 or 1890, and an organ sonata written in rather Mendelssohnian fashion, but which ended with three old hymns combined together in the coda.

An organ fantasia entitled *Variations on 'America'* was played in organ recitals in Danbury and in Brewster, New

Ex. 1. From Fugue in 4 Keys.

York, in 1891. This work contained pages his father would not let him play at the Brewster concert because they had canons in two and three keys at once that proved to be unsuited to performance in church: they 'made the boys laugh out loud and get noisy.' A little later the young composer wrote a fugue with the successive entrances of the voices each in a different key. When he showed the outline of this piece to his father, George Ives said: 'Charlie, it will be time enough to write an improper fugue and do it well when you can write a *proper* fugue and do *that* well.'

The year 1894 brought two experiences of the utmost gravity to the twenty-year-old Charles Ives, for he decided to continue his study of composition at Yale, and a month after his matriculation, his father died suddenly. George Ives was not yet fifty. Two years earlier he had given up the full-time profession of music for a job in the Danbury Bank, in the hope of finding greater security for his family; the decision undoubtedly influenced Charles Ives's later choice of a career. As the boy had fully expected to earn his own way through college, his father's death cannot have meant a great deal more hardship, but he missed his father intensely. George Ives's companiable enthusiasm for their common musical interests was a serious loss to a temperament little inclined to expose its intense feelings to the outside world.

One thing I am certain of, that if I have done anything good in music it was, first, because of my father, and second, because of my wife. What she has done for me I will not put down, because she will not let me.

But my father! — not only in his teaching from the technical side, but from his influence, his personality, character and open-mindedness, and his remarkable understanding of the ways of a boy's heart and mind.

He had a remarkable talent for music and for the nature of music and sound, and also a philosophy of music that was unusual. Besides starting my music lessons when I was five years old, and keeping me at it until he died, with the best teaching that a boy could have in Bach and the best of the classical music, and the study of harmony and counterpoint, he above all this kept my interest, and encouraged open-mindedness in all matters that needed it in any way.

For instance, Father thought that man as a rule did not use the faculties that the Creator had given him hard enough. I could not have been over ten years old when he would occasionally have us sing a tune like *Swanee River* in E-flat while he accompanied us in the key of C. This was to stretch our ears and strengthen our musical minds, so that they could learn to use and translate things that might be used and translated in the art of music more than they had been. In this instance, I do not think he had the possibility of polytonality in composition in mind, particularly; he rather wanted to encourage the use of the ears and mind to think for themselves and be more independent — in other words, to be less dependent on customs and habits.

I I I

College and Career

———

'THE INNATE REBELLIOUS SPIRIT,
ACTIVE AND BUOYANT'

When Charles Ives entered Yale, where three uncles, a
grandfather, and a great-grandfather had preceded him, he
got a job as organist of Centre Church on the Green. The
pastor was Dr. Griggs, an old friend of George Ives. By his
encouragement and unflagging interest in Charlie's musical
ideas, and by taking the boy to live in his home, Dr. Griggs
tried as best he could to take the place of his father. But of
course it was not the same thing.

In Horatio Parker's classes at Yale (where Ives spent four
years in connection with the regular academic course), ideas

of a musically exploratory nature were not so much suppressed as ignored. After the first three weeks Parker asked the boy not to bring any more things of the sort into the classroom, and to stick to the work regularly assigned to the class. Ives accepted this tractably enough, but he did occasionally try out a few things on the side — sometimes with the little orchestra in the Hyperion Theatre in New Haven, sometimes even at the organ in church.

Father had kept me on Bach and taught me harmony and counterpoint from a child until I went to college, and there with Parker I went over the same things even with the same harmony and counterpoint textbooks, and I think that I got a little fed up with class-room contrapuntal exercise, more because counterpoint was . . . too much of an exercise proper, instead of on the mountains.

I did sometimes do things that got me in wrong: for instance, a couple of fugues, with the theme in four different keys: C, G, D and A, and in another: C, F, B-flat and E-flat.

To show how reasonable an unreasonable thing in music can be: Look at a fugue! It is, to a great extent, a rule-made thing. So if the first statement of the theme is in a certain key, and the second statement is in a key a fifth higher, why cannot (musically speaking) the third entrance sometimes go another fifth higher? And the fourth entrance another fifth higher? And if it must hold to the nice old key system, why can't these themes come back in the same way?

'Because Bach did not do it,' Rollo says. Other reasons offered are not as good as Rollo's.

One Mus. Doc. says: 'Because it destroys tonality.' Now having four different men playing tennis together does not always destroy personality.

When all four keys got going at once, it resulted of course in the most dissonant-sounding counterpoint.

Parker took it as a joke; he was seldom mean, and I did not bother him much after the first few months — (but occasionally all the same). He would just look at a measure or so, hand it back with a smile, or joke about 'hogging all the keys at one meal,' and then talk about something else. I had and have ['great' crossed out] respect and admiration for Parker and most of his music. It was seldom trivial.

His choral works have dignity and depth that many contemporaries, especially in religious and choral compositions, do not have. Parker had ideals that carried him higher than the popular, but he was governed by the 'German rule,' and was in some ways somewhat hard boiled.

While he was at Yale, Ives wrote his First Symphony. It was supposed to be in D-minor, but the first subject went through six or eight different keys, so Parker made him write another first movement. He also felt the slow movement should start on F, not G-flat. The conclusion of the symphony was considered even more reprehensible, so at the request of Parker Ives wrote a 'nice' formal one. 'But the first ending is better!' he declares emphatically.

The new end part seemed no good to me and I told Parker that I would much prefer to use the first draft. He smiled and let me do it, saying: 'But you must promise to end on D-minor!'

[Parker's course] made me feel more and more what a remarkable background and start Father had given me in music. Parker was a composer, and Father was not; but from every other standpoint I should say that Father was by far the greater man. Parker was a bright

33

man, a good technician, but perfectly willing to be limited by what Rheinberger had taught him. After the first two or three weeks in Freshman year, I did not bother him with any of the experimental ideas that Father had been willing for me to think about and try out.

Among Ives's other teachers at Yale were H. R. Shelley and, for the organ, Dudley Buck.

The first 'serious piece away from the rule book' that now seems any good to Ives himself is an Organ Prelude and Postlude for a Thanksgiving Service, which he played in Centre Church in 1897. Horatio Parker 'made some fairly funny cracks about it,' but Dr. Griggs said it had something of the Puritan character, an out-doors strength, and something of the pioneering feeling. He liked it and told Parker so. Parker just smiled and took him over to Hueblin's for a beer.

> The Postlude starts with C-minor and D-minor together, and later major and minor chords together, a tone apart. This was to represent the sternness and strength and austerity of the Puritan character, and it seemed that any of the major, minor or diminished chords used alone gave a feeling of bodily ease which the Puritan did not give in to. There is also in this some free counterpoint in different keys, and rhythms going together. There is a scythe or reaping harvest theme which is a kind of off-beat, off-key counterpoint. Six or eight years later (sometime before we left 65 Central Park West in the fall of 1906), these 2 pieces were arranged as a single movement for orchestra.

This was the *Thanksgiving* music in the symphony *Holidays*.

It was while he was the organist at Centre Church that Ives got so tired of playing the same old hymns the same old way, with nothing but the tonic, dominant, and sub-dominant triads, that his fingers would occasionally balk in spite of his best intentions, inserting a dissonant note

Ex. 2. Organ interlude adding higher overtones
to chords in 'Nearer My God to Thee.'

of their own here and there. This was understandably complained of, but Dr. Griggs stood by him: 'Never you mind what the ladies' committee says,' he told Charlie, 'my opinion is that God must get awfully tired of hearing the same thing over and over again, and in His all-embracing wisdom he could certainly embrace a dissonance — might even positively enjoy one now and then.' In spite of an occasional flurry of complaint, Ives held this position till his graduation from Yale in 1898.

At Yale Ives seems to have been an active and sociable person. He was a member of HéBoulé, Delta Kappa Epsilon, and Wolf's Head. The four nicknames listed for him in the 1898 class book still seem to hit off various facets of his personality: Dasher (the spontaneous and explosive Ives); Lemuel (the ascetic New Englander); Quigg (the crotchety Quixote); and Sam (the punster and joker addicted to paradoxes). Besides writing music for fraternity shows (rather too much in accordance with his private ideas for the music to be liked — he was not mentioned in the musical account of his class in its yearbook) and playing ragtime with the little Hyperion Theatre orchestra for fun, he played on various football and baseball teams. Everything he did, he did hard.

He seems also to have made an occasional foray in the direction of literature. An article on the influence of Emerson was handed in to the Yale literary magazine of the time, and promptly handed back. Ives later incorporated this material into the chapter on Emerson in the *Essays Before a Sonata* (1920).

The leader of the Hyperion Theatre orchestra was a friend and Ives was able to try out short things with its players. Some of these pieces, conducted by himself, had several simultaneous rhythms and were written in more than one key. He liked to 'spell' the regular pianist, and would then sometimes improvise a dissonant, off-beat, or off-key accompaniment at the piano while the students sang or stamped out a march. They got so they liked these 'stunts' and would call for them. 'Now this may not be good evidence,' says Ives, 'but it shows what the ears can handle when they have to.'

As the end of his college career approached, young Ives was faced with the necessity of deciding how he should earn his living. To give all his time to music was a real temptation, but George Ives' son was only too well aware that a musician, no matter how practical a man he might be, would always have trouble providing for his family. Ives knew his own music to be anything but 'practical' and couldn't see where it was likely to be welcomed by anybody who would pay him for it. On the other hand he simply couldn't bring himself to write or play music he did not believe in. And although he was not to marry for another eight years, he never doubted but that he wanted the fullness of life instead of an ivory tower, and he looked forward to having a family of his own. So he decided against music, in favor of a business career.

Some ask me about, and apparently don't get it right, why and how a man who apparently likes music so much goes into business.

As a boy I was partially ashamed of music, — entirely wrong attitude but it was strong. Most boys in the country towns of America I think felt the same way. When other boys on Monday morning in vacation were out driving the grocery cart, riding horses or playing ball, I felt all wrong to stay in and play the piano. And there may be something in it. Hasn't music always been an emasculated art? Mozart helped too much.

Father felt that a man could keep his music interest stronger, cleaner, bigger and freer if he didn't try to make a living out of it. Assuming a man lives by himself and with no dependents, no one to feed but himself, and is willing to live as simply as Thoreau, he might write music that no one would play prettily, listen to or buy.

But — but if he has a nice wife and some nice children, how can he let the children starve on his dissonances? . . . So he has to weaken (and if he is a man he *should* weaken for his children) but his music . . . more than weakens — it goes 'ta-ta' for money! Bad for him, bad for music!

If music would not support him, he would have to go into business to support it. This was not so difficult a decision as it may seem, for Ives profoundly believed, with Emerson, that 'all things are One,' and that nothing else he might do need be really incompatible with creative work in music.

The next question was, what business? This choice was not to be left to chance by a young man whose aims for his life in general were no less staunchly exacting than for his music. His life work must fulfill his highest ideals by giving him the best possible opportunity to do the most good for the largest number of people. And it must be the kind of activity that had room at the top for men of originality, something with enough variety and scope for a man to get his teeth into and make himself felt.

To Ives it seemed obvious that the business of life insurance perfectly met these requirements. In 1898, when Charles Ives graduated from Yale, most people in the United States had been thoroughly convinced that the insurance companies were disinterested benefactors of the common man. So not long after Ivy Day, Ives went to New York to begin the 'practice of life insurance,' much as his classmates went into medicine or the ministry. He landed a job as clerk in the actuarial department of The Mutual Life Insurance Company, and his salary was $5 a week.

The actuarial department is the part of an insurance structure that keeps abreast of the statistical aspects of the business. The stability and success of an insurance company depend on the accuracy with which it calculates in advance the amounts it will have to pay out to policyholders. But because wars, epidemics, and the advances of medicine cause a constant revision of estimates, the business owes its indispensable factual foundation to the constantly revised figures of the actuaries. Ives calls this 'scientific,' meaning that the information derived in this way is based on the experience of a large number of people rather than on the opinions or estimates of a few. The actuaries' primary concern is the mortality table, which shows the effect on mortality of all the various aspects of human experience that affect large numbers of people at a time.

When Ives began his apprenticeship in the insurance business, the application of these statistics was still an expanding and exciting experience for a man with imagination. He was always more interested in the people behind the figures than in the figures themselves, so he did not remain an actuarial clerk very long. But his creative contributions to the insurance business could hardly have been made so successfully later if he had not had this early familiarity with the basis of insurance theory. He was at home with it from the first because his devotion to Emersonian doctrine led him to see, in the truths revealed by statistical averages, the expression of the Universal Mind, operating in the experience of many individuals.

With a group of young men his own age (one of them was Dave Twichell, brother of Charles Ives's future wife), the embryo insurance executive moved into an apartment on West 58th Street, between 8th and 9th Avenues, an apartment that its inhabitants promptly named Poverty Flat. Somewhat later the group of friends moved Poverty Flat to Central Park West. They combined to pay the expenses of running the place and the salary of a housekeeper who got dinner for them regularly. To increase his minute income, Ives then and for many years afterward acted as organist and choirmaster, first at the First Presbyterian Church in Bloomfield, New Jersey, and later at the Central Presbyterian Church on West 57th Street in New York (1899–1902). It was not unusual for Ives to recruit male voices from among his housemates, who were resigned to filling in even when they resisted permanent enlistment in the choir.

Charles Ives was long-legged, angular and wiry, with great nervous energy that often boiled up to the point of impatient explosion. The top of his lanky frame carried a small, high and narrow head, with strong features, capable of the most frowning intensity or the gayest challenging smile. He was a lively, bright personality, much sought after by his friends, who remember their own and his bachelordom as a period of ideal fun and freedom. Their wild oats were of a singular innocence, consisting mostly of nights spent playing ragtime in a beer garden or walking till daybreak in Central Park, afire with talk. 'More than once,' said a friend reminiscently, 'Charlie had just time to get out of his evening clothes before it was time to play the organ in church.' This seems to have been satisfyingly daring.

Always Ives was busy with composition in his free time. Ordinarily he got home from work about six-thirty and would arrive on the run, rush into the house, tear off his coat, collar, and vest, and hurry to the piano, where he would improvise and compose intently till he was called to supper. Afterward he would start thundering away at the piano again, singing to himself and scribbling hard, often until two or three in the morning.

On rare occasions he liked to crouch down behind the last row of seats in the balcony, with his back to the audience, like other students at Carnegie Hall before and since, to listen to the music of Beethoven and Bach. But on the whole he did little concert-going, since he found other people's music interfered with the music of his own that he was always carrying around in his head. Reminiscing around 1931, Ives wrote:

> I find that most musicians take it for granted that a man who composes music must, as a result, be conversant with all the music that has been written in the world up to last night . . .
>
> As I see it, there are two reasons why I do not. One is that, being in business for so many years, I had only evenings, Saturday afternoons and Sundays, and summer vacations of two or three weeks, in which to work. For this reason, as far back as 20 or 25 years ago, I got out of the habit of going to concerts, especially in

the evenings. I always seemed to have something I was working on and it was this, and the fact that my time was limited, that kept me from going out much.

Another thing, and I remember being conscious of this as far back as 1910 or 1911, after coming from a concert of the Philharmonic which I think Gustav Mahler conducted. On account of having only a limited time in which to work, I got into the habit of carrying things in my mind that were not put down or only partly put down on paper. As this was the case most of the time, I found that listening to music, especially if in the programs there were things with which I was not familiar, tended to throw me out of my stride. I will admit it may have been a kind of weakness on my part, but I found that listening to music seemed to confuse me in my own work — maybe not to a great extent but enough to throw me off somewhat from what I had in mind. Hearing the old pieces that I had been familiar with all my life, for instance the Beethoven symphonies, Bach, etc., did not, as I remember, have this effect.

At any rate, I found that I could work more naturally and with more concentration if I did not hear much music, especially unfamiliar music. To make a long story short, I went to very few concerts.

I suppose everyone is built differently and works differently! It just so happens that I felt I could work better and liked to work better if I kept to my own music and let other people keep to theirs.

Week ends offered some relief from the intensity of his life in New York. He and his brother Moss had a shack on a mountain top not far from Danbury, overlooking three valleys, and here he liked to camp alone, composing or just sitting, absorbed in the mountains. Then back to New York and the 18-hour days he imposed on himself.

Among the pieces Ives busied himself with at Poverty Flat was his Second Symphony. The last movement was 'the result of the Overture habit, common about two generations ago,' and had been played in Danbury by George Ives's orchestra in 1889. It incorporates a number of college songs. The Largo was 'a part from a revival service for string quartet, played in Centre Church (New Haven); but this was revised à la Brahms at Parker's suggestion.' Parker thought it was not dignified enough. *'But the first version was the best!'* This work was completed about 1902; it was scored later on, in 1909 or 1910.

At the same time he was at work on his Third Symphony:

> The themes are mostly based around hymns and from organ pieces played in Central Presbyterian Church around 1901. Lead pencil score was finished about 1901. But the final ink score (now lost) had I think a few of less off-shadow parts in it, and also church bells, that are crossed out in the old score . . . The middle movement was the *Children's Day Parade* (for string quartet and organ), played in Central Presbyterian Church, New York, for the organ alone, 1902. Scoring of this symphony was finished about 1904; copied out in full in 1911.

A program at the Central Presbyterian Church in April 1902 included a cantata, *The Celestial Country*, by Charles Ives. This seems to be the first performance of an Ives work to be accorded mention in the metropolitan press. *The New York Times* and the *Musical Courier* both reviewed it amiably; the latter calls attention to '. . . homogeneity . . . alternating 3/4 and 4/4 time measures . . . unusual harmonies, some complex rhythms, original ideas, effective part writing . . .'

About this time Ives decided he was doing too many different things, so he gave up his church job. After fifteen years at the organ on Sundays he found himself more exasperated than ever by the routine harmonies for hymns, and more and more inclined to vary them in his own way, sneaking up on the congregation with one or two dissonant notes until he was emboldened to accompany the hymn melody with its overtones, played far up in the treble of the organ. Somewhere along the line protests would arise, Ives would feel apologetic and return to convention, but not for long. Sooner or later the addition of sevenths of different sizes — major and minor — or a hint of another key or a syncopated rhythm would tempt him, and he would hope against hope that they would be inaudible to anyone but himself.

Always a deeply religious man, composition was for Ives a kind of spiritual practice even when it was not based on hymn melodies or connected in some way with church services. To go his own way, to write what he most honestly could believe to be beautiful and meaningful, was therefore a matter of conscience. As his music grew more and more unexpected to the average ear, he was presented with a dilemma.

And in playing [new music] at a service: — Is one justified in doing something which to him is quite in keeping with his understanding and feelings? How about the congregation, who were unused to the idiom, or rather to some of the sound combinations, and who might naturally misunderstand and be disturbed?

When a body of people comes together to worship, how far has a man a right to do what he wants, if he knows by so doing he is interfering with the state of mind of the listeners, who have to listen regardless and are helpless not to?

I seem to have worked (in composition) with more natural freedom when I knew that the music was not going to be played, at least publicly — or rather, before people who could not get out from under, as is the case with a church congregation . . . One has a different feeling in playing his music before an audience or a public that cannot help itself . . . In other words, a public audience, or a congregation, has some rights.

IV

Insurance Man

———

In the spring of 1899, Ives was transferred to the famous
Raymond Agency, then general agents of The Mutual Life
Insurance Company. Here he met Julian Myrick and the
two men became fast friends. Ives was full of ideas for im-
proving things in the insurance business, but there was
no machinery for getting the ideas of a five-dollar-a-week
clerk up to the men who might be capable of considering
his ideas for what they were worth. Instead, he was told so
often that 'the law made no provision' for something that
appeared to him both obvious and desirable that he entered night school in order to be able to refute his critics

with first-hand knowledge of the law. This put off composition till the late hours of the evening.

Along in 1906 Ives got very restless; he was tired of being under orders and felt he had too little scope for ideas of his own. He and Myrick spent the Christmas holidays of that year in East Hampton, and it seems to have been on that occasion that they decided to go into business together. So as of 1 January 1907, Ives and Myrick formed a partnership and secured for themselves a general agency with the Washington Life Insurance Company of New York.

Meanwhile, a more personal change was preparing in Charles Ives's life: he had fallen in love. Harmony Twichell was the daughter of Dr. Joseph A. Twichell, the Hartford minister who was Mark Twain's closest friend; she was one of nine children. The Twichell home was a center for a group of distinguished people during Harmony Twichell's girlhood — not only the Clemens family, who lived next door, but John Greenleaf Whittier, Charles Dudley Warner, and William Dean Howells were among her father's friends. When Charles Ives and Miss Twichell met, she was in training as a nurse in the old Presbyterian Hospital at 71st Street and Park Avenue. Her training completed, she went to work in Chicago, and young Ives got so apprehensive that life was a burden for his friends, for Harmony Twichell was a great beauty and he was convinced that his rivals were numerous. When she finally accepted him, everybody at Poverty Flat gave a sigh of relief. Not long before they were married Miss Twichell took Ives to call on the Clemenses at their New York house on lower Fifth Avenue. Mark Twain took it that the prospective bridegroom was being submitted for his approval and said genially, looking him over: 'Well, the fore seems to be all right; turn him around and let's see about the aft!' — a remark that Ives still enjoys repeating.

The marriage of Harmony Twichell and Charles Edward Ives was celebrated at Hartford on 8 June 1908, Dr. Twichell officiating, and the young couple set up housekeeping in New York City on a scale suitable to their modest circumstances. Ives, feeling deeply the increased responsibilities of a family man, applied himself strenuously to the affairs of the partnership. Not long after Ives's marriage, when the young partners had made what was generally considered a very successful start, their parent company sold its stock to another company which canceled the Ives & Myrick general agency so that the two men found themselves out of a job. Charles Ives still speaks of having to break the news to his wife as the toughest thing he ever did. 'What did she say?' he was asked, indiscreetly. After a long pause of reminiscence, Ives replied with the dry understatement that protects a New Englander's emotion: 'She didn't seem to mind.'

The horizon brightened almost immediately, however, for The Mutual Life Insurance Company, where Ives and Myrick had worked as clerks earlier, offered to open up an agency for the partners, making it clear that their energy and competence had already attracted favorable notice.

The partnership lasted until Ives's retirement from business in 1930. Calm, steady, and efficient, Julian Myrick was the perfect complement for the mercurial and creative Ives. Their long unbroken friendship is treasured by both men and when Ives is well enough the two families spend Christmas together. Of Ives as a business partner, Myrick wrote in 1947:

> Ives was not only creative in business but very practical and sound . . . He had a keen sense of humor and enjoyed a joke, although I do not remember his having much time to tell stories. His was a busy, hustling and active life as long as his strength lasted. All

of our agents, the people in the office and those associated with us had a great and undying affection for him. No one in trouble ever went away without good advice and sometimes substantial financial aid. He was completely unselfish.

Ives looked after the production, taking care of the agents' side of the business, and my activities were with the clerical, home office and outside contacts.

In our first year of business we paid for $1,800,000 and in the last, 1929, $48 millions. In the 21 years we were partners in the firm of Ives & Myrick, we put in force some $450 millions of new business for The Mutual Life of New York alone.

This was of great help to many policyholders, beneficiaries and the community at large, and also of great service to our field representatives. We had a live, active and progressive agency and, I hope, not only contributed our part to the growth and development of our own company but to the Cause of Life Insurance as a whole.

Myrick has always had great regard for Ives as a musician and he has seen to it that the insurance trade journals are informed of events in the music's career and of the honors that have come the way of its composer. For what is perhaps the most thorny of all Ives's pieces Myrick has a special proprietary affection:

We had a common safe, and when we moved from 37 Liberty Street to 38 Nassau Street, Ives had cleared his part of the safe and I was clearing mine when I came across a bundle of music in manuscript, which I thought he wanted thrown away . . . He came over and looked at it and said: 'My God, that's the best thing I've done yet.' It turned out to be the *Fourth of*

July for symphony orchestra — which, by the way, he says he is going to dedicate to me. I pointed out to him that his name would go down through the ages and as we had been partners and worked together for so long, I thought that my name should be associated with his in some way.

It was Julian Myrick who discovered during World War I that Colonel John McCrae, the author of a famous poem, 'In Flanders Fields,' was one of The Mutual Life's medical referees in Montreal, and it seemed logical to suggest that Charles Ives should set this poem to music. Myrick engaged professional performers to present it at a banquet of insurance men, but at the rehearsal they floundered through it in such a feeble way that the composer was depressed, and he told Myrick he thought they'd better just drop the whole damn project. The song is included in the volume *114 Songs,* dated 1919.

Only once did the two men have anything resembling a serious disagreement, whose course can be imagined from their expressed resolve never again to bring up the question of who did the most work. They are both generous men, and time and experience must have convinced them of the truth: that each man has been infinitely more effective because of the work of the other.

In 1949 Julian Myrick celebrated his 50th year in the insurance business, by which time he had become Vice President and General Manager of The Mutual Life Insurance Company of New York. The Ives & Myrick agency continues to function, under the management of Richard Myer.

There is no question but that Charles Ives was the right man in the right place as head of an independent insurance agency, but it is also true that the partnership was set up at exactly the right moment to take advantage of a period of great economic expansion in the United States, when conditions were particularly favorable for growth in the insurance business. As the form of our internal economy changed, insurance increased at a fantastic rate.

Toward the end of the 19th century the worship of size in American business reached its peak. In the insurance world, big companies, big buildings, big policies mushroomed in a self-congratulatory atmosphere, but it soon became evident that size did not necessarily mean security. Acute public criticism of the dangerously interlocking business structures that had become the rule provoked the Armstrong Investigation (1905–6) — a kind of an earthquake in downtown New York, which so shook the monumental insurance companies that veteran insurance men still refer to it as The Investigation, much as if it had occurred within the year. Its revelation of shamefully speculative practices resulted in a revision of the laws protecting policyholders, and forced the executives of the chastened big insurance companies to behave more circumspectly, as agents of the policyholders and trustees in the public interest rather than as powerful and arrogant tycoons intent on building individual fortunes.

The Mutual Life Insurance Company, with which Ives was to be associated almost all his business life, came off somewhat better than others in The Investigation, which some of its officers indeed encouraged. The reorganization that did take place installed as officers men who were conservative about expansion beyond the point of safety and careful about the investment of funds, so that a man of Ives's sensitive moral fiber could still feel hopeful about fulfilling the lofty aims with which he went into business.

Since the Armstrong Committee had concentrated its inquiry upon the pyramiding practices of the larger companies, many smaller concerns now felt encouraged to enter the field. This meant that competition was keener than it had ever been, providing a challenge well suited to Ives's temperament, for he enjoyed coping with the problems involved in combining expansion with economical administration, for one thing. New Englanders feel it a duty to get the most out of what they have to do with, and Ives is no exception.

Ives's belief in and concern for the common man led him to feel strongly about expanding insurance coverage to include more small policies from more members of low income groups. He felt it imperative that the number of people acceptable as risks be increased; and he also devoted himself with great energy and enthusiasm to unearthing new uses for insurance.

The writing of policies to meet specific needs of the insured was just beginning. Ives personally drafted the letters that were part of Ives & Myrick's promotional campaigns, and present-day public relations men go through the letters in which he solicited new business with a surprised respect, for the direct attack he used and the simplicity and clarity with which he makes his point are modern to the last degree — as different as possible from the oratorical tone that characterized publicity and promotion at that time. The events of his own life suggested his points of attack: young husbands were reminded to protect their wives' futures, and when in 1910 Mr. and Mrs. Ives adopted a baby girl named Edith, her father began to suggest that his clients look ahead to insure their children's education by an insurance policy. Businessmen (and business women, whose existence was not taken seriously by most men at that time) were urged to anticipate a variety of losses, and to keep pace with increased income by increased insurance so that calamity would not bring about too sudden and severe a change in their families' standard of living. In 1918 Ives had a serious illness, and this suggested a new field: his promotion letters inquire about the prospect of comfortable retirement in the event of illness or old age.

Insurance men today remember Ives chiefly for two things. One is the organization of the Ives & Myrick training school for agents, which was imitated all over the country and became an indispensable part of every large insurance company. The other is the concept of 'estate planning,' which was Ives's own idea; it is nowadays considered basic in the life insurance business.

The success of the system for training insurance sales agents that Ives established grew out of his awareness that the most effective selling technique was to make the prospect come to the agent instead of the other way around. Confident that what his agents had to offer was something the prospect needed and wanted whether he knew it or not, Ives concentrated on making insurance salesmen into educational, not sales, agents. It was characteristic of Ives's thinking, in whatever field, that a plan of action should be based on 'the big things' — the broad, general principles of life and the facts about it — and he trained his agents to suggest a revision of the prospect's basic thinking about financial security and protection, letting details fall into line of themselves. Odd though this must have sounded at first in downtown New York, phrased as it was in the style of the Concord philosophers, it created a new and immensely successful jiu-jitsu technique of salesmanship. A prospect was confronted with a questionnaire; when the blanks were filled out with the figures about his present income and possible resources in the event of crisis, the discrepancy in protection practically always forced him to sell himself more insurance. The agent didn't even need to know the exact figures.

Not the least important aspect of this idea was the ease with which it could be made clear enough to be taught methodically to new agents and put into practice at once. Because Ives believed insurance to be 'an expression of a fundamental human need,' he never doubted that providing for this need was a contribution to the development of mankind in general and insurance agents in particular. And as a developing, useful man is a happy man, Ives took great satisfaction in thinking that the sale of life insurance on these principles was for the good of the salesmen's souls as well as their pocketbooks.

This was a period when Ives was as active in music as he was in business, completing or composing his most strenuous and striking musical works at night, after long days spent in downtown New York under the full pressure of the big business world. After he finished the *Concord Sonata* in 1915, he began to gather together and amplify the notes that were to accompany it and which eventually became the little volume he called *Essays Before a Sonata*. But this was not his first published literary work.

In 1912, two years after the initiation of the Ives & Myrick training school for agents, the firm printed a booklet entitled *The Amount to Carry — Measuring the Prospect*. This soon became the Bible of insurance agents; its author was Charles Ives. It has been reprinted many times, parts of it are still frequently quoted, and the clear and simple principles it crystallized into statement for the first time are now widely in use.*

* In October 1953, one of the authors had an animated neighbor on a bus between Kingston and New York who introduced himself as an insurance lawyer engaged in outlining proper estate insurance for his clients. Estate insurance proved to be something devised 'by a famous insurance man of a past generation named Ives.' This gentle-

The Amount to Carry was intended as a handbook for insurance agents, but one may read through the first three sections and most of the fourth, almost 2000 words, without finding salesmanship mentioned once. A note under the title admits frankly: 'The subject matter relating to practical agency work begins in Section IV, part 4.' Up to this point Ives carries forward his instruction on the broadest Transcendental lines, outlining a kind of social history of the concept of insurance.

> There is an innate quality in human nature which gives man the power to sense the deeper cause, or at least to be conscious that there are organic and primal laws . . . underlying all progress.
> The instinctive reasoning of the masses has been the impelling influence in social progress; the intellect has been subordinate . . . perhaps because the premises, or the lessons from the deeper impulses have not been universally distributed, hence only the few have been able to observe them, and the many have not. But as the truer premises are becoming more widely distributed, the major intellect grows in power to appreciate them; superstition is giving way to science.
> The cause of so much interest in the superficial which remains in our political life is due . . . to this same insufficient premise distribution. The Minority Mind has been too timid to trust the Majority Mind and hence reluctant to pass around the facts.

The 1922 edition of *The Amount to Carry* appeared at

---

man was astonished to hear that Ives wrote music and to be shown the title page of this book and a fragmentary music manuscript. He had some literature with quotations from Ives's insurance pamphlet in his pocket. The writer was pleased to be assured afresh that the insurance business is 'a natural form of expression for an idealist.'

George Edward Ives, 1845-94, father of the composer, in his uniform as leader of the Brigade Band of the First Connecticut Heavy Artillery during the Civil War, photographed about 1862.

Charles Edward Ives, captain and pitcher of the Hopkins Preparatory School baseball team which defeated the Yale freshmen in 1894.

a time when Ives was devoting a great deal of thought to political conditions in the United States and so a parenthesis at this point offers, to anyone asking for it, a copy of a proposed constitutional amendment that he devised to increase active participation in government by the largest possible number of citizens. Then he goes on to point out:

> The improvement in service and increase in efficiency, nowadays, in most lines of business, is but an evidence of this gradual progress in learning how to discard the superficial for the fundamental. That is, a greater number of essential truths . . . are being observed by a greater number of minds.

Under the heading 'Life Insurance Doing Its Part,' the author remarks that his readers will probably be more bored by all this than interested, but he continues in the same strain:

> [In the distribution of insurance] an emotional appeal to the moral and altruistic side of human nature had to start men in overcoming prejudice and in accepting . . . a social duty. [But] this period is fast closing. As its functions [those of life insurance] become more and more a matter of common knowledge, the need for emotional processes becomes less and less.

After expressing a hope that emotional processes won't be weeded out entirely because they contribute so much color and variety to thinking he concludes Section II:

> It can be said . . . that the development of life insurance, particularly in the manner of presenting its services to the public and in increasing the benefits, has become more and more scientific in its work. That is, the fundamental in each essential premise has become clearer and clearer to more minds. *Life insurance*

is doing its part in the progress of the greater life values.

Part III is devoted to outlining the 'growth of insurance intelligence,' a growth due, he feels, to those 'persistent distributors of premises,' the pioneer agents of earlier generations, who 'pounded out the "gospel," perhaps only crudely, and with methods more emotional and personal than we have to use today.'

This leads naturally to Part IV, 'Ways to Build Production':

Agents as a rule fail to show the client the kind of reasoning he, the average prospect, is looking for . . . There seems too often to be . . . more stress on the 'psychology' of a sale than on the 'science' of it, that is the fundamental reason for it . . . an over-appeal to the weakness of the average personality, and an under-appeal to the strength of the average mind.

Once this, his principal point, is successfully made, Ives follows with sections headed concretely: 'Measuring Insurance Needs'; 'Inadequate Conception of Insurance Amounts'; 'Formula for Determining Necessary Average'; 'Productive Periods'; 'When There Are Two Children or More.'

With 'Twenty Opening Suggestions' Ives stands beside his agent-to-be at the door of the prospect's office; for example:

I want to talk life insurance to you for four minutes. I want to tell you something no agent has ever told you. I can answer scientifically the one essential question. Do you know what that is?

Or, if especial resistance is anticipated:

My company has recently worked out an answer to a question about life insurance that has been asked for 40 years and never answered. Do you want to know what that is?

And (recommended to house-to-house canvassers for small policies):

Does your wife spend too much for clothes? or Is your wife making her end of the business pay?

Then come 'The Prospect's Objections'; 'The Agent's Answers'; 'Calculating with Pad and Pencil' (not in the prospect's presence); 'If He Debates, Your Hold on Him Is Growing'; 'The Matter of Cost' (tell him frankly and go on to something else); 'Domestic Inefficiency' (use of The Mutual Life's cost-of-living chart); 'Plan [of interview] Should Be Rehearsed'; and, under the heading 'Not Complicated,' Ives concludes his training pamphlet with a statement that he acted upon consistently in all his own affairs:

Whoever takes the trouble to know what he has to know . . . in as perfect a way as he is capable, and then keeps at it until all sides of his problem become as clear to him as the sun was to Galileo, that man will find a way of making his message clear to the dullest listener. Truth always finds a natural way of telling her story, and a natural way is an effective way, simple or not.

Once his newly fledged agents emerged from training school and were hard at work each in his own territory, they were peppered intermittently with memoranda from Ives's pen. For instance:

At the end of each day write out the presentation that you have found the most effective. Eliminate the waste processes and make the strong ones stronger!

And:

April, May and June! New Problems, New Possibilities!

Or:

At a time like this, the more prospects an agent sees the more he makes the law of averages work in his favor. To be more concrete, if an agent wrote 25 cases in 1915 and averaged 8 interviews a day, the same interview average will bring him 32 cases this year. If he concentrates and forces himself up to 12 interviews a day, he will double last year's amount. He increases his energy by one-half but doubles the results.

Again, to new agents:

When Wordsworth said that he could write like Shakespere if he had a mind to, Charles Lamb replied: 'Yes — the mind is the only thing lacking.'

During the last part of 1915 renewed activity was felt everywhere . . . The Mutual Life agent never started the year with more in his favor, so if he cannot increase his business in 1916 it will be because 'the mind is lacking.'

Coming upon this form letter in an old Ives & Myrick scrapbook at The Mutual Life offices, one of the authors commented in pleased surprise: 'Now who would ever have thought of quoting Wordsworth and Lamb to insurance agents?' 'Not me,' returned Julian Myrick cheerfully from across the big office. 'That was always Charlie.'

And finally this one, also addressed to agents:

Don't bluff. You don't have to. An agent of only 3 months' experience knows more about life insurance than most prospects. The wisest actuary can't answer off the bat every technical question that is thrown at him. If doubtful, say you'll bring back accurate information, and then swing into the BIG things, there are plenty of them. If you can't make your prospect like you or your policy, make him like Life Insurance anyway. Knock some BIG ideas into his mind. Every man wants to be independent and have his family independent. That's the spirit of America and of humans in general. Nothing can help a man more than the thing you have for him: Life Insurance.

Carefully preserved in the historical collections of The Mutual Life's library is a fifteen-page memorandum written by Ives about 1920, just after the *Essays* were completed and while the *Concord Sonata* was going through the press. It is the longest of a series addressing officials in his particular peppery fashion. 'We are all conscious of the Company's virtues,' he remarks, 'but to dwell on them constantly doesn't necessarily help to increase them.' And: 'If good prompt service is desirable, why not give it instead of reasons why things cannot be done that should be done?'

This memorandum begins by urging more frequent exchange of information and more active participation in policy decisions by a larger proportion of the Company's staff. More information about the higher-level thinking and executive decisions should be distributed downward from the trustees and officers to the agency managers and agents. And more suggestions should reach the president and the trustees from the people in contact with the public.

A life insurance agency is a financial institution: Why are there no more than five members on the Finance Committee? Broaden the base!

A life insurance agency deals with many kinds of problems: Why are the trustees men primarily concerned with business, and other business at that, not insurance? Wouldn't it be better to have a few technical specialists on the board, men familiar with medicine, public health, economics, public welfare, advertising, mathematics?

And why not a dyed-in-the-wool insurance man for president, a man with 'an instinctive judgment in insurance matters'? Why was the president (to whom, it should be remembered, these animadversions are directed) chosen from outside the ranks of insurance men? Surely his difficulties have been the greater because he was not 'inherently' an insurance man. 'He has not been especially progressive,' adds Ives, warming to his subject,

> . . . and he has not realized, perhaps, the full possibilities of The Mutual Life and Life Insurance as an institution . . . because he is not a man who has been trained in the fundamental experiences of Life Insurance.

Next, Ives takes up the subject of administrative deficiencies and urges, apparently not for the first time, the appointment of another vice-president to co-ordinate and expedite the business of the various offices.

> But when the Managers' Committee, two years ago, interested themselves in the matter and took the proposition directly to the Board of Directors . . . no one said so in so many words, but we were given to understand that in making our appeal in this matter, we were but playing politics, that the agents were trying to run the Company, and so on. But if it is playing politics to express a conviction, if it is playing politics to seek a way of increasing the Company's benefits to society, then I say, let's play politics!

Such an executive would free the second vice-presidents to devote their time to the larger problems of extension, research, and liberalization of the Company's services.

For instance, says Ives, waxing indignant again, in the Medical Department, the Company is about 10 years behind in its attitude towards many things. Why shouldn't the Medical Department know at once the result of any contemporary research? It seems to me that in the selection of risks there is too much stress put on the impression of one man. A more scientific determination seems possible.

The individual opinion of one man, or of one company, for that matter, is becoming less and less valuable. The total experience of all companies points a way to wider service and incidentally to a better mortality. There *must* be some better way of measuring risks than has yet been devised, but this method will probably not be evolved until there is a more systematic and constant co-operation of all Medical Departments.

The companies are quick enough in knowing what risks other companies turn down. Why shouldn't they be as quick in finding other things of greater importance? Why shouldn't they be as interested in trying to find out why some of the bad risks are *good,* as why some good risks are *bad?*

Again . . . in the selection of risks from an occupational standpoint, there is room for progress . . . The Company is not especially enthusiastic about many classes of laborers which it ought to accept. We ought to study a way to bring them to us, but it is difficult for the agent to do this if he is conscious of a prejudice on the part of the Company. Personally, I would rather have on the books a thousand stevedores at $1,000 each than ten bank presidents at $100,000 each. The apparent advantages to the Company of the latter group (if any) would in the writer's opinion be a small item, compared with the value to the Company of being in touch with and in an intimate position to render service to the future generations of these thousand men.

The force of the last argument is superb, and explains why Charles Ives was a real figure in the insurance world. If a man whose philosophy of life commits him to work for the greatest good of the greatest number finds his way into a business for which a broad base is of the first importance, and if he can formulate a simple proposition that will oblige the forces of custom and convention to match his idealism because their profit so plainly depends on their doing so — such a man will be as creative and effective in business as any artist.

The memorandum to President Peabody has a disarming conclusion:

Quite naturally, anybody who may hear all this may say: 'How about the writer? Is he all virtue? Is he so efficient that he can criticize in this easy way?' No! that is the worst of it, he isn't. But Mr. Baxter keeps us on our toes, and unfortunately there are others in the Company who don't have this stimulus! So the writer subscribes to the foregoing for what it is worth — and remains in a receptive mood toward anyone who wants to take a crack at him.

V

The Professional World of Music

'THE OPPORTUNITY
OF NOT BEING OVER-INFLUENCED'

The period of Ives's most strenuous devotion to his business was also the period of his most energetic creative production of music. He was no split personality, but functioned as the same whole man wherever you find him, with a fine flow of creative energy that crystallized and organized business ideas into new relationships just as it did his musical ideas at home in the evenings.

In 1910 Charles Ives was thirty-six years old. His face had lost its boyish roundness and seemed narrower, to match the long spare frame on which his clothes hung loosely and, like Lotring, another composer halfway around the world, in Bali, 'his hair had grown thin thinking of music.' Ives had been married for two years, his business was soundly established and growing, and it was in this year that his household was completed by the happy addition of a baby daughter named Edith.

For the next eight years Ives was to function with his energy and imagination at their height, initiating and carrying out his special contributions to life insurance and to music alike. During the years of his liveliest business activity he wrote music practically every evening, turning out page after page of sketches that he made a habit of tossing over his shoulder into a confused pile of sheets on the floor. Completed drafts of large works went into the pile too, and the stacks of sheets have never been thoroughly sorted out to this day. Occasionally a work was copied out in full by Ives himself or turned over to a copyist, a Welshman named Price, who was a thorn in the composer's side because of his not unnatural insistence on understanding what he was doing. Nothing can have prepared him for the sights that met his eyes, and nothing seems to have prepared Ives for Price's inevitable dismay.

There was small inducement to set all the music in final form, however, because no performances seemed likely, so Ives gave his musical imagination full rein. Most of his music was made in a state of fine creative excitement and satisfaction, for he believed that 'to speak adequately, he must speak wildly, with the flower of the mind,' as Emerson has it, 'abandoning himself to the nature of things and letting the tides roll through him.' Small wonder if even his most appreciative critics have found crudities and incongruities and awkwardness in the music. No composer so aware of the endless possibilities could be expected to arrive at the ultimate statement of every musical idea.

The list of works produced during these eight years of greatest energy is prodigious for so short a period; for the evening and week-end production of a busy man it seems hardly credible. For the symphony *Holidays* he rescored the *Washington's Birthday* movement (1913) and completed *Decoration Day* and *The Fourth of July* (1912–13); he composed all of the Fourth Symphony (1910–16) and a number of pieces for various instruments, some with voice or chorus: *The New River,* for example (1912), *December* (1912–13) and *General William Booth's Entrance into Heaven* (1914). In 1911 he put in order his *Set for Theatre or Chamber Orchestra,* parts of which date from 1906 and which has some ragtime bits in it; the three parts are called *In the Cage, In the Inn,* and *In the Night.* He completed his First Orchestral Set (1906–14), called *Three Places in New England,* or sometimes *A New England Symphony,* whose three movements are *Boston Common, Putnam's Camp,* and the famous *Housatonic at Stockbridge;* * and he composed all of a Second Orchestral Set (1912–15), likewise in three movements: *An Elegy, The Rockstrewn Hills Join in the People's Outdoor Meeting,* and *From Hanover Square North, at the end of a tragic day, the Voice of the People again arose.* For string quartet and piano he wrote a Hallowe'en piece in 1911, the same year that he composed the *Browning Overture* for orchestra; the whole of his Second String Quartet was written between 1911 and 1913. He completed his Second Violin Sonata (1903–10) and his Third (1902–14) and wrote all of the Fourth (1914–15),

* The last movement, *The Housatonic at Stockbridge,* was suggested by a Sunday morning walk that Mrs. Ives and I took near Stockbridge the summer after we were married. We walked in the meadows along the River and heard the distant singing from the Church across the River. The mist had not entirely left the river bed, and the colors, the running water, the banks and trees were something that one would always remember.'

which is subtitled *Children's Day at the Camp Meeting.*

In 1914 he arranged some old quarter-tone pieces for two pianos. The next year he completed his best-known work, the Second, or *Concord,* Sonata, for piano, in four movements: *Emerson, Hawthorne, The Alcotts,* and *Thoreau.* And at intervals during most of this time (1911–16) he worked on his *Universe Symphony,* 'the underlying plan of which was a presentation and contemplation in tones, rather than in music as such, of the mysterious creation of the earth and firmament, the evolution of all life in nature and in humanity to the Divine.'

Since Ives was composing or completing a number of things he himself found especially interesting, he made his first — and only — attempts to introduce the music to musicians who might play it, and to friends who might make the effort to understand it. The autobiographical notes contain many an unhappy reference to criticisms, by friends and others, and Ives has set down a surprisingly complete record of their effect on his music, even listing works he believes were adversely affected.

Dave [David Stanley Smith] and Max Smith were old friends of mine, and real friends at that, men I respected and got along with, except when it came to music. Max Smith and Mary spent one Sunday with us in May 1912 or 1913 at the Whitman House in Hartsdale. I played over the Third Symphony and Max asked how I had 'got so modern. It's even worse than 10 years ago!' Then I played over the Black March (St. Gaudens) which I was working on then, and some of the brass band stuff in Putnam Camp, and some of the Hawthorne music, and one particular spot in the Fourth Symphony. After I finished, Max, who had gone out on the stoop, said: 'That first one was bad enough, but these were awful! How CAN you like horrible sounds like that?' Max at that time had been for a good many years the music critic on the N.Y.American. And Dave, like a lot of other professors in colleges, would have agreed with the violinist Reber Johnson, who once lay back and groaned: 'Music is now a lost art; it is going to the dogs.' Professors who take that stand are exactly like a Professor of Transportation who teaches all about steam and refuses to admit that any things exist such as electricity or combustion engines.

Another time Reber said to me, after I had played over for him the Second Violin Sonata (that harmless little piece!): 'Stuff like that . . . ! If you consider that music and like it, how can you like Brahms and any good music?' So! If you like the one, you can't like the other! This is as much as to say: 'If you look out of this window and enjoy the mountains, how can you possibly look out of *this* window and enjoy the ocean?' [In the margin Ives has commented to himself: 'This is a very good simile!']

Some time in 1910 a business acquaintance, rather against Ives's better judgment, persuaded Walter Damrosch to try over parts of the First Symphony at a rehearsal of the New York Symphony Orchestra. Ives thought he was taking sufficient precautions against too violent protest from the musicians when he refrained from offering Damrosch the first movement (since its combinations of keys had not pleased Horatio Parker), suggesting instead the second movement. What Ives badly needed, as a composer, was to hear what he had written come to life. He wanted to know whether his music sounded the way he thought it did, and if he himself liked it, above all.

The pages in his autobiographical notes that described this bitterly frustrating experience have disappeared; they were probably taken out and destroyed upon rereading. What Ives now remembers is the pleasant initial impression of an attractive tune, which made Damrosch call out: 'Charming!,' then the total inability of the orchestra to keep going, and the frequent stops to correct what Damrosch cavalierly assumed, without reference to the composer, to be wrong notes. At a passage where duple meter in one part appeared with triple meter in another part (a device that could hardly have been really startling, since it was already familiar in the music of Chopin, Schumann, and Brahms), the conductor called out patronizingly: 'You'll just have to make up your mind, young man! Which DO you want, a rhythm of two or a rhythm of three?'

The *Washington's Birthday* score was tried over, shortly after it was written, by a few theater orchestra men who had been persuaded to come to a back room at Tam's Copying Bureau. It was also played twice in the Globe Theatre, in 1914 and 1915, after hours, probably at Ives's expense. As usual, not all the instruments were present, but Ives felt they got through it fairly well. Later another personal friend, Reber Johnson, then assistant concert master of the New York Symphony Orchestra, brought a group of men to the Ives's apartment at 120 East 22nd Street to try over the same piece.

> These were supposed to be the best men in the orchestra, and they were good musicians, but the Globe Theatre orchestra did as well, if not better. They made an awful fuss about playing it, and before I got through, this had to be cut out, and that had to be cut out, and in the end, the score was practically emasculated. After 6 or 8 rehearsals it was approximately well played, but only after some of the parts which

seemed to me the strongest and the best were cut out. Harmisch, the viola player, was the only one who was not more or less mad at the trouble the music gave them. He suggested that the piece be played at one of their concerts, but Reber Johnson answered: 'No, we must think of the audience.'

Edward Stowell, director of the orchestra of the Music School Settlement in West 3rd Street, once drove over to Hartsdale to call on Ives. Stowell noticed the score of the *Fourth of July* music on Ives's desk, and picking it up he declared roundly: 'This is the best joke I have seen for a long time! Do you really think anybody would be fool enough to try to play a thing like that?' The two men tried over Ives's Second Violin Sonata and began to read through the First, but Stowell found it too hard and stopped; he said there were too many ideas too close together. They next tried over what was then the most popular work for violin and piano by an American: Daniel Gregory Mason's Sonata. Stowell informed Ives that the reason Mason's Sonata was better than his was that Mason wrote *Geiger Musik* (fiddle music, that is, music composed to sound well on the violin without too much trouble). Ives mulled over this remark for years and wrote at length in answer to it in his *Essays Before a Sonata*. However, he was elated at the time to have Stowell say that there were more ideas on one page of his Sonata than in the whole of Mason's. (Later on it occurred to him that this was probably meant as a recommendation to restraint and prudence, and he was correspondingly depressed.) Finally, Ives showed Stowell a part of his Second Symphony which could be played by string orchestra; Stowell liked this much better and conducted it at one of the Music School Settlement concerts. This work was to wait nearly forty years longer for its first complete performance. Distressed at the rejection of Ives's music by other musicians, a friend was impelled to ask why Ives didn't write music people might like. Ives answered him in equal distress: 'I can't do it! — *I hear something else!*'

One of the few bright spots in Ives's account of his attempts to get people to try his music over so he could listen to it was a friend named David Talmadge, a violinist who tried out several of Ives's violin sonatas with the composer. 'He gave them serious, hard and intelligent study, and he played them well and in a kind of big way,' said Ives. In 1917 Talmadge and Stewart Ross played one of the sonatas for an audience of invited guests at Carnegie Chamber Hall.

Ives's old friend, Frank Kaltenborn from New Haven, once played over for him parts of the Theatre Orchestra set, and Ives suggested to him that he play it at one of his St. Nicholas Rink concerts. He replied, much like Reber Johnson, that he'd be very glad to play it, but he didn't want to lose all his New York backing, so felt he had better not. Another time, Bass Brigham, 'Yale '97 and a violinist,' called on the Iveses at 70 West 11th Street, when Ives was scoring *The Housatonic at Stockbridge*. 'Well, that is a funny collection of sounds. Your tonality and your chord relation is more wobbly than Cesar Franck's, which is bad enough!' Ives felt himself to be writing *music,* not 'tonality' or 'chord relations' as laid down in the theory books he and Brigham had studied at Yale, and was deeply resentful. These experiences eventually convinced him that he should retire from the professional musical arena, and led to the dry remark, in *Essays Before a Sonata:* 'Everyone should have the opportunity of not being over-influenced.'

Such detachment was of course a counsel of unattainable perfection. Actually these periodic blows to his self-confidence had a kind of 'sedative effect,' and Ives felt that 'most often, after these incidents, nothing happened, good or bad, which is good.' He sometimes returned for several months to conventional ways of writing, until he got so tired of it that he felt, 'I would either have to stop music or stop this.' In a mood of honorable confession, Ives lists pieces marked, to his mind, by such retrogression: 'For instance, some of the songs in 1908–09–10 are in this kind of a slump. The songs called *Evidence* (58), *Autumn* (60), *Nature's Way* (61), *The Waiting Soul* (62), and *Spring Song* (65) are samples; so is the string quartet around 1905–06 (mostly destroyed later or worked into something else); some other pieces for strings; the Third and Fourth Violin Sonatas. The First Violin Sonata too, though in some places it is quite the opposite. Most of the pieces written in this state of mind I can spot every time I look at the first measures.' The songs *Serenity* (42) and *Old Home Day* (52) are included in the list of 'slumps,' above, but the composer seems to have changed his mind and decided they are not as bad as he thought at first, for he has crossed them off.

The Third Violin Sonata (sometimes referred to by Ives as the Fourth until he finally decided that the first one he wrote did not deserve to be counted) * was begun as an organ piece in 1901 and finally finished in the fall of 1914. Ives remarks of it that the older it got the worse it got.

This Sonata is a good example of the result such experiences with people trying over my music sometimes had. The last movement especially shows a kind of

* This indecision resulted not only in two First Violin Sonatas, a complete one that Ives now includes in the four he has numbered and published, and another earlier one that lacks its intended third movement and is identified as the 'pre-First,' but also in several years of confusion as to which of the violin sonatas he is talking about when he refers to them by number. Recently an incomplete movement of an even earlier sonata came to light; Ives called it 'a start toward a violin sonata' and said it was made earlier than his 'pre-First' one.

reversion; the themes are well enough but there is an attempt to please the soft-ears and 'be good.' The Sonata on the whole is a weak sister.

Elsewhere he refers to this same piece as 'a slump-back,' and goes on to explain that this is due, he feels certain, to a visit made to his West Redding home in 1914 by 'a typical hard-boiled, narrow-minded, conceited, prima donna solo violinist with a reputation due to his coming to this country from Germany with Anton Seidl as concert master.' He continues:

Mrs. Ives had known him in Hartford, and as I had had so much trouble with musicians in playing my music, we thought it would be a good plan to get one of the supposedly great players. Before finishing the Third Sonata, I wanted to have the First and Second played over.

Well, the 'professor' came and after a lot of big talk he started to play the first movement of the First Sonata. He didn't even get through the first page. He was all bothered with the rhythm and the notes and got mad. He kept saying: 'This cannot be played . . . This is awful . . . It is not music, it makes no sense.' Even after I had played it over for him several times, he could not get it then. I remember he came out of the little back music room with his hands over his ears and said: 'When you get awfully indigestible food in your stomach that distresses you, you can get rid of it. But I cannot get those horrible sounds out of my ears with a dose of oil.'

What Ives calls 'masculine language,' a good God damn now and then, and other much more imaginative cussing, is frequent in his own speech; but the vulgarity of such comment on music deeply and sincerely conceived was profoundly shocking to him.

After he left, I had a kind of a feeling which I have had, on and off, when other celebrated musicians have seen, or played, or tried to play my music. It was only temporary, but I did for a while feel that there must be something wrong with me. Said I to myself: I am the only one, with the exception of Mrs. Ives and Ralph D. Griggs, who likes any of my music — except perhaps some of the older more conventional things. Why do I like to work in this way and get all set up over what just upsets other people . . . ? No one else seems to hear it the same way. Are my ears on wrong?

The composer's single support during this period of abortive attempts to get a hearing for his music was Mrs. Ives. She remained uncompromisingly sure that a creative person must seek his whole justification in himself, no matter how his work appears to others. If he is right about its value, recognition will come; if wrong, he still can't hope to achieve anything by being anybody but himself.

I am going to put this down after those musical friends of mine, mentioned above: Mrs. Ives never once said, or suggested, or looked, or thought that there must be something wrong with me — a thing implied, if not expressed, by almost everybody else, including members of the family. She never said: 'Now why don't you be good and write something nice the way they like it.' Never. She urged me on my way to be myself and gave me her confidence that no one else since Father had given me.

A free translation of most of the general advice that I

always received from musicians, friends and otherwise, and also from personal and family friends was: 'If you want something played, write something you do not want played.' Mrs. Ives always said the opposite, and resented the above (free translated) advice.

During the years when Ives made occasional attempts to have his work performed, there was nobody else so far ahead of current usage in America. What he wrote seemed natural and inevitable to him, as any creative effort does to its producer. The maddening inadequacy of early performances and the derision of the performers turned Ives back upon himself and he retired, not without some profane expostulation, to work alone, though with diminished energy. 'I began to feel that if I wanted to write music that was worth while (that is, to me), I must keep away from musicians.' His isolation increased his concentration upon the music of the Ideal, of the Transcendental, music that was to be uninhibited by the limitations of people and instruments, satisfying to the composer even if unheard.

An element in the situation peculiar to Ives's life was the extent to which he was isolated from other creative spirits engaged in the same kind of struggle. His marriage and his business life cut him off from the Bohemian world of musicians where he might have encountered rumors about other equally scandalous music. He had no way of knowing what Arnold Schoenberg was going through at about the same time in Vienna. Fifteen years or so later, through *New Music,* Ives was to find friends and allies in other composers, but the sense that he was not alone was unhappily conveyed to him too late for effective encouragement, for by that time he had stopped writing music.

V I

Ives Cleans House and Retires

———

'ALL THAT IS LEFT
IS OUT ON THE CLOTHES LINE'

A retrospective paragraph in Ives's autobiographical notes makes it clear that his actively productive period as a composer ended with the First World War in 1917–18. The war was a shock of the first magnitude to a man whose life was based on his confidence in human progress. His first serious physical breakdown came a month before the war's end, and it seems to have closed the door on further sustained creative activity.

[My] . . . things [were] done mostly in the twenty years or so between 1896 and 1916. In 1917, the War came on and I did practically nothing in music. I did not seem to feel like it. We were very busy at the office at this time with the extra Red Cross and Liberty Loan drives, and all the problems that the War brought on. As I look back, I find that I did almost no composing after the beginning of 1917. In October, 1918, I had a serious illness that kept me away from the office for six months, and I have not been in my former good (very good) state of health since . . . nor have I seemed to 'get going good' in music since then. I'd start things but they didn't seem to work out, so I stopped. I do not know how to account for it except that during the last 10 years (since 1918) what strength I had was used up in what I had to do at the office — and then the War — and it seemed impossible to do any work in the evenings as I used to do. During the last 10 years or so I have completed nothing; a set of chamber music was started and is fairly and mostly set down in a sketch some five or six years ago; and I have started a Third Pianoforte Sonata, which does not seem to get along very well. In 1919–20 and especially 1921 I did write a few songs, and also at that time made arrangements of songs from old sketches, scores, overtures, etc. [Written about 1928.]

His illness, which left him with permanent cardiac damage, gave him much time for reflection, and Ives revised his idea of what he should do about his music. As soon as he was well enough, early in 1919, he resolved that whatever he had written that he felt was entitled to see the light of day should be printed and sent out to make its own way, if it could. The world of music specialists — the narrow professional world of conductors and performers — was obviously closed to him and his ideas. He would let his music appeal instead, if it could, to 'the average man who is Humanity.' Ives may well have read, in *Walden:* 'The true husbandman will cease from anxiety . . . and finish his labor with every day, relinquishing all claim to the produce of his fields, and sacrificing in his mind not only his first but his last fruits also.'

He decided to make the world a free gift of whatever it could use in what he seems to have felt was his 'more accessible' music, and it was because he thought that songs and piano music were more likely to be tried over by 'the average person able to tinker a little at the keyboard' that he had the *Concord Sonata* and the *Essays Before a Sonata,* and a little later the volume called *114 Songs,* privately printed and distributed without copyright and free of charge; no one was expected or allowed to pay for them. They were sent to libraries, music critics and musicians, and to anybody else who asked for them. He also began to have duplicate photostat copies made of all his manuscripts, a project that continued over many years.

In a postscript to the *114 Songs* Ives addressed the 'gentle borrower' of the volume: 'Some have written a book for money; I have not. Some for fame; I have not. Some for love; I have not. Some for kindlings; I have not . . . In fact, I have not written a book at all — I have merely cleaned house. All that is left is out on the clothes line . . .'

Composers never seem to consider their music at all difficult to understand, but even so it is odd that Ives thought his most characteristic songs would be comprehensible to the average singer; and it is really extraordinary that he should have believed that the *Concord Sonata* might be accessible to the ordinary pianist. John Kirkpatrick devoted years to unraveling its meaning a good many years later. Ives seems to have considered that performers were deliberately recalcitrant when faced with his music, that they *could* have grasped the music but were unwilling to make the effort. He thought the average man or woman at the keyboard might be more open to new ideas. In a way he was right, but a great part of the trouble was inherent in the situation. Prophets are never immediately comprehensible in their own time; if they are, they are not prophets.

The published volume of songs seemed to Ives, upon consideration, to include too many things he felt were of no special value except as exercises or 'trial balloons,' so in 1923 he chose fifty of them for a smaller edition. Still later, the songs omitted seemed perhaps not so bad after all, so he had the original edition reprinted.

Ives found texts for his songs not only in the poetry of Keats, Browning, Stevenson, Robert Underwood Johnson, Walter Savage Landor, Louis Untermeyer, and so on, but also in poems (always left unsigned) by his wife. Now and then he composed a kind of Whitmanesque prose poem for himself, also unsigned. There are bits of incredible doggerel for 'take-offs' on popular ragtime ditties. Many of these texts have the same homely quality as his quoted melodies, but he does not use them as a jumping-off place for further development. His formal imagination is not apparently stimulated by words as it is by musical ideas; he is prodigal of inner rhymes and alliteration, and when he repeats a furious prose sentence for emphasis, the climax seems to be achieved by shouting rather than construction.

There are settings of Italian, German and French poems, and a number of appealing songs that use only a phrase or two from some longer poem, often eloquent or nostalgic in their brevity. All the songs were dated and printed as first written. Permission to use a poem of Kipling's that he had set never came, so he printed the song with Kipling's title (*Tarrant Moss*) and the first few words; a singer can fit the remainder in without difficulty. Perhaps the most extraordinary pieces in this Gargantuan collection are *The Majority*, a massive affair intended to be sung by a single voice or by a unison chorus against thickly filled dissonances in the piano, and a long song about an election called *November 2, 1920*, which begins: 'It strikes me that . . .': this is a sardonic comment on the ease with which, in the author's opinion, the United States turned its back on a high purpose when it deserted Woodrow Wilson and the League of Nations.

Some of the songs, such as *The New River* and *Lincoln, the Great Commoner*, appealed to Ives particularly, and he later made them into larger pieces using various combinations of instruments. Other songs moved in the other direction, out of larger works into the *114 Songs*. Among these is a group of four songs that are based on old hymn-tunes, two of which were used in the Second Violin Sonata, one in the Fourth, and one in the Third Symphony. The short vocal versions contain sly notations of the vagaries of congregational singing, where a hymn is likely to go slower and slower and flatter and flatter in pitch. Ives has written the rhythms as they are actually sung, the notes of the melody dropping farther and farther behind the regular beat which is kept up by the piano. Where the voices let the pitch drop, he has written a change of key.

As a footnote to one of a playful set of sentimental songs, Ives expresses the hope that it will never be taken seriously, nor sung, at least in public. And of the second song in a group of five street songs, Ives writes:

This song (and the same may be said of others) is inserted for association's sake — on the ground that that will excuse anything; also, to help clear up a long-disputed point namely: which is worse, the music or the words?

The song in question, *In the Alley,* was written in 1896 after a session at Poli's; it is one of Ives's ragtime pieces. In the seventeenth measure, next to a well-behaved C-major chord there is a tiny parenthetical chord turning the harmony into a banal dominant seventh on C, and a note says: 'Use Saturday night.' The fifth measure is arranged so as to free one hand for the regular pianist at Poli's (George Felsberg) to turn the pages of the newspaper he habitually read while playing. At the end a note over two broad arpeggiated chords says: 'Change swipe ad lib.'

> George could read a newspaper and play the piano better than some pianists could play the piano without any newspaper at all. When I was in college, I used to go down there and spell him a little if he wanted to go out and get a glass, or a dozen glasses, of beer. There were black-faced comedians then ragging their songs. I had even heard the same thing at the Danbury Fair before coming to New Haven, which must have been before 1892 — [Ragging was] throwing the accent on the off-beat and holding over, — a thing that so many people nowadays think was not done until jazz came along.
>
> If one gets the feeling . . . of these shifts and lilting accents, it seems to offer other basic things not done, or done very little, in music of even beats and accents; at least, it seems so to me.

The *114 Songs* forms the most original, imaginative, and powerful body of vocal music that we have from any American, and the songs have provided the readiest path to Ives's musical thinking for most people. Many of them have a touching lyrical quality; some are angry, others satirical. The best of them are musically very daring, with vocal lines that are hard for the conventionally trained artist, accompaniments that are often frightfully difficult, and rhythmic and tonal relations between voice and piano which require real work to master. Even when the melodic line alone presents no special problem, in combination with the accompaniment it offers a real challenge to musicianship. Surmounting the difficulties of this music creates an intensity in the performer that approaches the composer's original exaltation and has brought audiences to their feet with enthusiasm and excitement. But the simplest and least characteristic of the songs are still the most often performed. Like Schoenberg, whose fame rests on musical usages that had not yet appeared in the early pieces ordinarily offered on concert programs, Ives has been represented, as a rule, by pieces that have little or nothing to do with the music that made his reputation.

The *Essays Before a Sonata* was designed to accompany the *Concord Sonata* (No. 2 for piano), as an elaborate kind of program note (124 pages long); it was finally printed separately only because the combination proved too cumbersome. The music was written between 1909 and 1915; the essays were put in order during Ives's long convalescence after a breakdown in 1918, but they had occupied his mind for many years before that. The final form of the book seems to have been settled while Ives was recuperating in Asheville, North Carolina, in 1919.

Even before he left Yale Ives had been writing about Emerson. On their honeymoon in 1908 Mr. and Mrs. Ives had visited Concord, and they repeated the trip the year before Ives's first serious illness: the family photograph album contains several dark and nearly indecipherable photographs in which Charles Ives can just be made out standing by Walden Pond, at the site of Thoreau's cabin and before the grave of Emerson.

Ives has always had a real gift for expressing himself in vivid and unconventional ways. William Lyon Phelps wrote accurately of the *Essays* that they were the result of 'chronic cerebration' and he recommended them to those 'who have brains and wish to use them.' The *Essays* do not explain the music; they demonstrate the mind that made it.

Along with the ardent flood of ideas in its prologue and epilogue, the volume has a chapter of reflections upon each of the four 'wise men of Concord,' to whom Ives had devoted a movement of his sonata: Emerson, Hawthorne, Alcott, and Thoreau. The first words to catch one's eye stand alone:

> These prefatory essays were written by the composer for those who can't stand his music — and the music for those who can't stand his essays; to those who can't stand either, the whole is respectfully dedicated.

Then the prologue begins:

> How far is anyone justified, be he an authority or a layman, in expressing or trying to express in terms of music (in sounds if you like) the value of anything, material, moral, intellectual, or spiritual, which is usually expressed in terms other than music? How far afield can music go and keep honest as well as reasonable or artistic? . . . Does the success of program music depend more upon the program than upon the music? If it does, what is the use of the music, if it does not, what is the use of the program? . . . On the other hand, is not all music, program-music — is not pure music, so-called, representative in its essence? . . . Where is the line to be drawn between the expression of subjective and objective emotion? It is easier to know what each is than when each becomes what it is.

The chapter on Emerson, 'a great poet and prophet . . .

greater, possibly, as an invader of the unknown,' is an ardent flow of freely associated ideas, often so involved in expression (because Ives floods his sentences with the opposite of his thesis, with parentheses and the contrary of his parentheses, and with queries whose chief excuse for being is their play on words) that one easily fails to discover where the writer is going until the very end. He would rather have the reader share his experience than follow a well-constructed description of it. Writing in defense of Emerson's style, Ives manages to say just what might be offered in defense of his own:

> Nature dislikes to explain as much as to repeat. It is conceivable that what is unified form to the author, or composer, may of necessity be formless to his audience . . . Initial coherence today may be dullness tomorrow, probably because formal or outward unity depends so much on repetition, sequences, antitheses, paragraphs with inductions and summaries.

At the end of the chapter Ives suddenly emerges into unqualified statement:

> Within [Emerson's] poised strength, we are conscious of that 'original authentic fire' which Emerson missed in Shelley — we are conscious of something that is not dispassionate, something that is at times almost turbulent — a kind of furious calm lying deeply in the conviction of the eventual triumph of the soul and its union with God!
> There is an 'oracle' at the beginning of the Fifth Symphony — in those four notes lies one of Beethoven's greatest messages. We would place its translation above the relentlessness of fate knocking at the door . . . and strive to bring it toward the spiritual message of Emerson's revelations — the Soul of humanity knock-

ing at the door of the Divine mysteries, radiant in the faith that it *will* be opened — and the human become the Divine!

Of Hawthorne and Alcott he writes briefly: he describes the second movement of the Sonata as an extended fragment that ignores the fundamental melancholy and consciousness of evil in Hawthorne, trying only to suggest some of his 'wilder, fantastical adventures into the half child-like, half fairy-like phantasmal realms . . . music about something that never will happen, or something else that is not'; and of his third movement he says:

> We won't try to reconcile the music sketch of the Alcotts with much besides the memory of the home under the elms — the Scotch songs and the family hymns that were sung at the end of each day, with a strength of hope, a conviction in the power of the common soul . . .

Ives begins with Thoreau resoundingly:

> Thoreau was a great musician . . . The rhythm of his prose, were there nothing else, would determine his value as a composer. He was divinely conscious of the enthusiasm of Nature, the emotion of her rhythms and the harmony of her solitude . . . In their greatest moments the inspiration of both Beethoven and Thoreau express profound truth and deep sentiment, but the intimate passion of it, the storm and stress of it, affected Beethoven in such a way that he could not but be forever showing it and Thoreau that he could not easily expose it.

He disputes Thoreau's critics one by one, more warmly even than he did the detractors of Emerson. Someone called Thoreau idle; if this person had just had more brains, Ives

declares violently, you could call his statement a lie. Such
a man is the kind who 'plays all hymns, wrong notes, right
notes, games, people and jokes literally and with the pedal
down, who will die literally and with the pedal down.'
Even the men who wrote most eloquently of Thoreau do
not entirely suit Ives:

You, James Russell Lowells! You, Robert Louis
Stevensons! You, Mark Van Dorens! with your literary
perception, your power of illumination, your bril-
liancy of expression, yea, and with your love of sincerity, you know your Thoreau, but not *my* Thoreau —
that reassuring and true friend, who stood by me one
'low' day when the sun had gone down long, long before sunset . . .
If there shall be a program for our music let it follow
his thought on an autumn day of Indian summer at
Walden . . . a shadow of a thought at first . . . a
certain restlessness, an eagerness for outward action
. . . he sets off along the beach, but with these faster
steps his rhythm is of shorter span, it does not bear the
mood that the genius of the day calls for, it is too
specific . . . too external . . . too buoyant. He re-
leases his more personal desires to Nature's broader
rhythm, conscious that this blends more and more
with the harmony of her solitude; it tells him that
his search for freedom on that day, at least, lies in his
submission to her, for Nature is as relentless as she is
benignant . . . He realized what the Orientals meant
by contemplation and forsaking of works . . . his
meditations interrupted only by faint sounds . . . the
evening train, the prayer-meeting bell in Concord, the
vibrations of the wind through the trees . . . It is
darker, the poet's flute is heard out over the pond, and
before ending his day he looks out over the clear,

crystalline water of the pond and catches a glimpse of the shadow-thought he saw in the morning's mist and haze . . . He goes up the pleasant hillside of pines, hickories and moonlight to his cabin, 'with a strange liberty in Nature, a part of herself.'

The Epilogue is the longest part of the book; its nine sections are related rather as the parts of a starfish are related: attempts at parallels lead one toward a point that grows ever more distant from the last point, and any attempt to return leads one across the center to the opposite of the initial statement. If one can just abandon preconceived notions of the way ideas should be arrived at, it makes rewarding reading. For instance, Ives begins with a series of rhetorical queries about the possibility of program music: What the composer intends to represent as 'high vitality' may sound very different to different listeners . . . A child can distinguish between a strain of joy and one of sorrow . . . those older, between dignity and frivolity, between spring and autumn,

> But where is the definite expression of spring against summer, of happiness against optimism? . . . But maybe music was not intended to satisfy the curious definiteness of man. Maybe it is better to hope that music may always be a transcendental language in the most extravagant sense. Possibly the power of literally distinguishing these shades of abstraction is ever to be denied man for the same reason that the beginning and end of a circle are to be denied.

A good many pages in the *Essays* are devoted to the distinction between manner and matter in the arts and in the course of this discussion there are fragments that reveal Ives's opinion of certain composers.

A young man, two generations ago, found an identity

feel certain, a strong help to me in future work — I can stand any ~~amount~~ amount of "adversity" from an open and thoughtful mind.

Mrs. Ives & I, are looking forward to seeing you, and Mrs. Bellamann, in Newport this winter. We hope you will get there without fail.

    Sincerely
    Chas. E Ives.

Aug 28 -21.

    I have now sent x tra copies of your October, Southwestern, New Orleans. I presume just this address will reach them.

Last page of a letter from Charles Ives to Henry Bellamann in 1921, acknowledging a copy of the first review of the *Concord Sonata* and asking for a fuller expression of opinion about the music from Bellamann's 'open and thoughtful mind.'

Charles Edward Ives about 1910, at the height
of his business activity and musical creativity.

with his ideals in Rossini; when older, in Wagner. A young man one generation ago found his in Wagner, but when older in Cesar Franck or Brahms . . . an experience we believe to be normal. (The author) remembers, when he was a boy of about 15, hearing his music teacher (and father) who had just returned from a performance of *Siegfried* say with a look of anxious surprise that 'somehow or other he felt ashamed of enjoying the music as he did,' for beneath it all he was conscious of an undercurrent of make-believe — the bravery was make-believe, the love was make-believe, the passion, the virtue, all make-believe . . . But that same boy at twenty-five was listening to Wagner with enthusiasm; the reality was real enough to inspire a devotion. The *Preislied,* for instance, stirred him deeply. But when he became middle-aged, this music had become cloying, the melodies threadbare — a sense of something commonplace, yes, of make-believe came. These feelings were fought against for association's sake and because of gratitude for bygone pleasures — but the former beauty and nobility were not there, and in their place stood irritating intervals of descending fourths and fifths. Those once transcendent progressions, luxuriant suggestions of Debussy chords of the 9th, 11th, etc., were becoming slimy. An unearned exultation . . . hides around in the music. Wagner seems less and less to measure up to the substance and reality of Cesar Franck, Brahms, d'Indy or even Elgar (with all his tiresomeness); the wholesomeness, manliness, humility and deep spiritual, possibly religious, feeling of these men seem missing and not made up for by Wagner's manner and eloquence.

Writing 15 years later Ives tempers this judgment slightly:

Richie Wagner did get away occasionally from doh, me, soh, which was more than some others did. He had more or less of a good head for technical progress, but he seems to put it to such weak uses, exulting . . . in fake nobility and heroism, but afraid to jump in a mill-pond and *be* a hero. He likes instead to dress up in purple and sing *about* heroism. Music has been, to too large an extent, an emasculated art, and Wagner has done his part to keep it so. What masculation he has in it, is make-believe.

Even today probably about 83% of the so-called musical programs lean more to the mollycoddle than the rough way up the mountain.

In the *Essays* Ives compares Debussy to Thoreau:

Debussy's attitude toward Nature seems to have a kind of sensual sensuousness underlying it, while Thoreau's is a kind of spiritual sensuousness. It is rare to find a farmer or peasant whose enthusiasm for the beauty in Nature finds outward expression to compare with that of the city man who comes out for a Sunday in the country, but Thoreau is that rare country man and Debussy the city man with his week-end flights into country esthetics.

On Tchaikovsky:

Some claim for Tchaikovsky that his clarity and coherence of design is unparalleled (or some such word) in works for the orchestra. That depends, it seems to us, on how far repetition is an essential part of clarity and coherence. We know that butter comes from cream, but how long must we watch the churning arm? If nature is not enthusiastic about explanation, why should Tchaikovsky be?

In the autobiographical manuscript, Ives made other plain remarks about composers:

> Most of Chopin is pretty soft, but you did not mind it in him so much, because one naturally thinks of him with a skirt on him, but one which he made himself.

> It seems to me today as it did 35 or 40 years ago, and ever, that still today Bach, Beethoven and Brahms are among the strongest and greatest . . . I will not say that their best is better or worse than anything in any art, before or since — I will not say, because I do not know, and nobody knows (except Rollo).

Ragtime was new and exciting in New York when Ives was young but he recognized that it came straight from minstrel show music. It was already a familiar ingredient in vaudeville music when he was in college. By the time he was writing the *Essays* there had been some attempts to show that since Brahms and Schumann had used syncopation it could not be considered American.

> To examine ragtime rhythms and the syncopation of Schumann or of Brahms seems to the writer to show how much alike they are not. Ragtime, as we hear it, is, of course, more (but not much more) than a natural dogma of shifted accents, or a mixture of shifted and minus accents. It is something like wearing a derby hat on the back of the head, a shuffling lilt of a happy soul just let out of a Baptist Church in old Alabama. Ragtime has its possibilities. But it does not represent 'America' any more than some fine old senators represent it. Perhaps we know it now as an ore before it has been refined into a product. It may be one of Nature's ways of giving art raw material. Time will throw its

vices away and weld its virtues into the fabric of our music.

And about American music he says elsewhere in the *Essays:*

> If a man finds that the cadences of an Apache war-dance come nearest to his soul, and provided he has taken pains to know enough other cadences (for eclecticism is part of his duty: sorting potatoes means a better crop next year), let him assimilate whatever he finds highest in the Indian ideal, so that he can use it fervently, transcendentally, inevitably, furiously, in his symphonies, in his operas, in his whistlings on the way to work . . . this is all possible and necessary, if he is confident that they have a part in his spiritual consciousness. With this assurance his music will have everything it should of sincerity, nobility, strength and beauty, no matter how it sounds . . . true to itself, and incidentally American . . . American even after it is proved that all our Indians came from Asia.

The Epilogue ends with humility:

> The strains of one man may fall far below the course of those Phaetons of Concord — but the greater the distance his music falls away, the more reason that some greater man shall bring his nearer those higher spheres.

The three published volumes — *Sonata, Essays,* and *Songs* — were well made, and it was the fate of many of them to be used to adjust the height of the piano bench in the studios of more than one of the best-known musicians of the day. This led to a series of obvious and vulgar jokes, in which connection many musicians, among them Henry

Cowell, heard Ives's name for the first time. Sensitive as Ives was to criticism, however, he still cherished the hope that somewhere the music would find its welcome if he could get it into the right hands. His Emersonian philosophy and his experience of the insurance business combined to convince him that the 'law of averages' would discover his audience for him if only he distributed his music widely enough. Eventually he was to be proven right about this, but for another twenty years the hope seemed vain.

The interruption of other musical work to prepare these three volumes for publication, and the inhibiting effect of the wave of laughter the music provoked, are more than enough to account for the ensuing period, until 1927, during which Ives might still have written a great deal of music, but did not. He started two new works that seemed to lead nowhere and were left unfinished — a third piano sonata, another orchestral set. He sketched out instrumental settings for a few of the songs and piano pieces and then turned for a while to other things.

He did a great deal of literary scribbling, and undertook to get onto paper some of the ideas — economic and political ideas as well as musical ones — that were boiling up in him, in a spirit of ardent expostulation with the *status quo* in all these fields. His furious creative embrace of the insurance business necessarily slackened somewhat long before he resigned formally, but he was far from idle, for he undertook the vigorous propagation of ideals he shared with Thoreau about building the nation on fundamental truths instead of the selfish ideas of a powerful minority. For many years, Ives has constituted himself a one-man political movement.

Never a man to come to some general intellectual conclusion without concrete suggestions for implementing it,

Ives made proposals in his many political papers that are surprisingly precise. In one of them, a long document entitled 'The Majority,' begun in 1912 and finished about 1922, Ives covers a wide range of economic and political ideas, arrived at quite alone by applying Transcendental thinking to his personal experience.

'The Majority' is primarily an appeal for more direct participation by every man and woman in solving the problems of government. Ives's scheme for bringing this about suggests the New England town meeting on a national scale: any citizen may bring up anything he considers important on a preliminary 'suggestive ballot.' The duty of Congress is to classify these suggestions by subject and separate the fundamental from the minor (as indicated by the topics of interest to the greatest number of people) for presentation at an election that will decide what is to be done about each issue. The ballots for this second election are to contain clear, concise but full arguments on *both* sides of every question. Just as a healthy stomach puts food to the right use if it has the right kind of food, so the Majority Mind will come to the proper decision about questions that concern it if the right mental food (facts, specialists' data, etc.) is presented to it. 'If one won't admit that, he comes pretty near admitting that God is incapable,' says Ives bluntly.

What Ives was trying to do was to devise machinery for bringing to bear on the questions that most plague the average citizen (financial security, industrial peace, foreign war), that Universal Mind, or Oversoul, declared by Emerson to be the source of all effective thought and action. As soon as Ives became aware that representative government did not always work perfectly, it seemed a duty to ponder a scheme that would make the state operate more nearly in accordance with the laws of nature as expounded by the Sage of Concord. Evolution was obviously a law of nature, an expression of progress arrived at through the operation of the 'divine law of averages,' of which as an insurance man Ives had had so intimate an experience. So he declared that if enough men and women expressed themselves on any issue, the majority would be right and would, moreover, be able to reconcile the extreme views of minority groups by insisting on all the facts until the solution became self-evident.

Just after the First World War, when the quarrels engendered by Wilson's campaign for the League of Nations were acute, Ives was convinced that such a union of the world's peoples was the only possible bulwark against war. As a child he had accompanied his father to a reunion of Civil War veterans at Gettysburg, and he never forgot an old Confederate soldier who said that it wasn't *his* war: if anybody had asked *him,* no guns would have been used to back up arguments. Ives felt that an overwhelming majority of citizens would agree with this if they knew all the facts and had a chance to register their opinion, and so he formulated a suggested 20th Amendment to the Constitution, based on the conclusions he had arrived at in 'The Majority.' This was designed to make possible the more direct type of election, with votes taken on issues, not on individuals. He had this printed and distributed it as widely as he could, to members of Congress and all State Legislatures, and to anyone else who asked for it or who he thought might be interested.

Ives makes no apology for his concern with economic security. Spiritual values may be paramount, but they cannot operate when their pathway is 'clogged up with unnatural economic arrangements.' As early as 1907, when he first went into business for himself, it had occurred to him to wonder what each individual's share in the total wealth of the United States would be, if an individual maximum were set above which personal wealth could not go, and the surplus evenly divided. Ives interested the treasurer of the Washington Life Insurance Company in the idea and they arrived at some figures: Suppose the maximum allowable annual income were set at $7500, everybody (each wage earner or family head) would have $900 as a starter toward making that maximum. Of this idea he wrote:

> A system under which each man had a minimum Natural Property Right recognized as his share in majority possessions, with the possibility of working to increase this as his initiative and the needs of his family suggest to him, up to an agreed maximum which would be high enough to encourage individual action but low enough so as to rob nobody of his minimum share, has the good points of both the 'isms': capitalism and communism.

This concept of the individual's relation to the wealth of his country under a democracy governed Ives's own behavior when his firm began to make a great deal of money; he limited his own income to what he calculated an individual's share of the country's wealth should be, taken in relation to the rights of other citizens. The surplus, which in Ives's case was large, was returned to the business. Ives believed a man who had a great deal more money than his neighbors was in moral danger, and he pointed out that too rich manuring of the ground is as damaging to crops as too little.

All his life he has been accustomed to carry forward some aspect of Emerson's or of Thoreau's thinking in terms of present problems, checking whatever conclusions he arrived at against what he has observed of 'science' and 'natural laws' operating in the insurance business, in music, and in Nature. If he could find a sufficient number of analogies in these various fields, he was satisfied he was on the right track.

This was a process that went on entirely in his own head, however. It had nothing to do with any set of economic ideas as expounded by the various radical groups of the time. He rejected socialism, syndicalism, communism, and anarchism as urgently as he did capitalism, for he felt they represented 'minority thought' and that a solution acceptable to the Majority Mind lay elsewhere. He once undertook to read some much talked-of economic treatises, but they struck him as polemical, out to talk other men down rather than to inquire for the truth; their insistence put them under suspicion and he discarded them. He was more interested in inquiring how many men's ideas could be heard as a preliminary to effective conclusions and action. 'A greater share in decisions for everybody concerned in them! and see to it that the largest possible number ARE concerned!'

Ives's precarious health made him less and less able to attend to business affairs, and after 1927 he seldom went down to the office. His first trip abroad with his family in 1924 had improved his condition somewhat, but by 1930 it became apparent that he would not be able to return to the insurance business, and so he decided he must retire from the partnership of Ives & Myrick. It was both touching and embarrassing when Julian Myrick inserted a tribute in the advertising pages of the leading trade journal, *The Eastern Underwriter* (19 September 1930). This was headed: 'What the Business Owes to Charles Ives' and was signed by Myrick.

When Charles E. Ives retired from active participation in the Ives & Myrick Agency of the Mutual Life a few months ago the insurance fraternity of Greater New

York lost contact with a guiding spirit whose impress upon his fellows was stimulating, uplifting and of untold value to insurance production. His creative mind, great breadth of culture, intensive sympathies and keen understanding of the economic as well as of the material needs of the community made it possible for him to evolve literature which paved the way for additional sales of life insurance and helped straighten out complications which confront the underwriter in his daily path through life.

This remarkable student, seated in his Connecticut home with pen in hand, has loved to concentrate upon and to analyze the problems with a master mind. Always shall I be proud and happy in the recollection of our partnership of twenty years' standing, not only because of its intimate nature but no one had a better opportunity than was mine of knowing how great was his contribution to the cause of life insurance progress. In my opinion that contribution has never been properly assayed or acknowledged. The passing years will demonstrate that his philosophy will ever hold good.

A little later Henry Bellamann asked how a composer could have reconciled himself to the demands of a business career, and Ives replied with his famous philosophical synthesis of music and business:

My business experience revealed life to me in many aspects that I might otherwise have missed. In it one sees tragedy, nobility, meanness, high aims, low aims, brave hopes, faint hopes, great ideals, no ideals, and one is able to watch these work inevitable destiny. And it has seemed to me that the finer sides of these traits were not only in the majority but in the ascendancy. I have seen men fight honorably and to a finish, solely for a matter of conviction or a principle — and where expediency, probable loss of business, prestige or position had no part and threats no effect. It is my impression that there is more open-mindedness and willingness to examine carefully the premises underlying a new or unfamiliar thing, in the world of business than in the world of music.

It is not even uncommon in business intercourse to sense a reflection of a philosophy — a depth of something fine — akin to a strong sense of beauty in art. To assume that business is a material process, and only that, is to undervalue the average mind and heart. To an insurance man there *is* an 'average man' and he is humanity.

I have experienced a great fulness of life in business. The fabric of existence weaves itself whole. You cannot set an art off in the corner and hope for it to have vitality, reality and substance. There can be nothing *exclusive* about a substantial art. It comes directly out of the heart of experience of life and thinking about life and living life. My work in music helped my business and work in business helped my music.

VII

The Career of Ives's Music

'IT CAN STAND AND IT CAN GO'

Composers are born, but a career is always made. Even the greatest music has always had to establish itself through the interest and effort of many people who are able to forward it. To the extent that they are convinced by it and believe in it, the music may be said to make its own way, but contrary to the general notion, fame never arrives untouched by human hands.

The first stage in the career of Ives's music came to an end about 1918 when he decided to make no further personal effort to introduce the music to performers who had shown no interest in it, but to send the three published volumes out to make their way as best they could. Thereafter Ives helped his music toward performance or publication only when someone else sought him out to suggest it.

With hardly an exception at first musicians ignored the *Concord Sonata*, the *Essays* and the *Songs* or else commented tartly or with condescending wit. There was one man, however, to whom Ives's music and his writing about it made an immediate appeal, and who remained its devoted friend to the end of his life. This was the poet Henry Bellamann, later famous as the author of *King's Row*, who was writing about music and lecturing in the South when he received the *Essays*, and the *Sonata*. Sometime in 1919 he began to write about Ives in southern newspapers and journals, about the strange new shape of his music and what he thought music might be. To illustrate his lectures on music Bellamann persuaded Lenore Purcell, an exceptionally gifted young pianist who must have been exceptionally venturesome as well, to tackle the *Concord Sonata* in public in New Orleans in October 1920. She gave performances of it, usually one movement at a time, in conjunction with Bellamann's lectures, across the southern states from New Orleans to Spartanburg, South Carolina. It was her performance in New Orleans that was reviewed under the headline: 'A Terribly Hard Taste of Music.'

Bellamann wrote Ives and after some correspondence was invited to call on him at his office when next he came to New York. This Bellamann did, only to be told by a secretary that without an appointment he could not see Mr. Ives for two weeks. She was finally persuaded that Bellamann was there at Ives's request and took his name in, with a hint to be brief.

He found Charles Ives sitting in an immense room, behind a huge and highly polished desk that was completely bare.* It required a moment's conversation to persuade him that this was indeed Ives the composer. But once talk about music began, Bellamann couldn't get away, in spite of his best intentions, for over three hours. Later in the day, still a trifle dazed at the impact of so surprising a personality, he mentioned to another Wall Street business-man, a banker, that he had spent the entire morning with Charles Ives, and this man stared at him: 'Why you liar! Nobody gets three hours of Charles Ives's time, he's head of the biggest insurance agency in the country.'

Mr. and Mrs. Ives invited the Bellamanns to visit them at West Redding, and, put off by a mistaken sense of Wall Street grandeur in the Ives's background, Mrs. Bellamann nearly told her husband to go alone, feeling she had no adequate clothes for the occasion. This amuses her greatly in retrospect, for their tall, thin, bearded host came to meet them in the battered hat and old corduroy jacket he still often wears, and she found that nothing could be simpler than the style of living of the Ives family.

Mrs. Bellamann was a concert singer of real distinction, and she gave Ives one of the great pleasures of this period of his life when, sometime in the mid-'twenties, she over-came the difficulties of a number of songs that he had about decided could never be sung. He was surprised and excited; 'Why, they sound just like I thought they would!' he ex-claimed over and over, in incredulous delight.

* This is what Mrs. Bellamann remembers of her husband's account. On the other hand, all other evidence suggests that Ives was not a model efficient executive, and that his desk was always littered with papers. Probably both descriptions were perfectly accurate at differ-ent times. He detested the necessity for a receptionist, wishing to be available to anybody at any time. By the time Henry Cowell met Ives a couch had been added to the furniture of the office so Ives could lie down whenever his excited marching about the big room brought on an attack of breathlessness.

The music was to be introduced to a very different world at about the same time, through a happy accident. In 1924, the French pianist E. Robert Schmitz went into the office of Ives & Myrick in search of an insurance policy. Like Bellamann, he spent the better part of a day in conversation about musical experiment with the surprising man with whom he had planned to talk about business. Schmitz was deeply impressed with Ives's personality and interested by his ideas on music, and it seems to have been owing to a suggestion from him that Ives and Hans Barth met and temporarily combined their efforts on behalf of quarter-tones. In the course of his concert tours about America, Schmitz had founded the Franco-American Music Society (later called Pro Musica), a network of regional music clubs which became famous for its promotion of modern French music. A concert of quarter-tone music arranged by Hans Barth under its auspices was given in Town Hall in February 1925; included were three pieces by Ives.

The quarter-tone concert aroused a great deal of laughter both then and later, but Schmitz was not discouraged. The next year a referendum was held by Pro Musica to determine the neglected composers whose music people were most curious to hear, and the name of Ives turned up among them. So when Pro Musica's International Referendum Concert was held at Town Hall on 29 January 1927, an orchestra work by Charles Ives was presented for the first time to a sophisticated musical audience in New York. This consisted of two movements (the prelude and the second movement, in which a few quarter-tone chords are used) from the Fourth Symphony, then called Symphony for Orchestra and Pianos; the program notes were written by Bellamann and the conductor was Eugene Goossens.* The

* Darius Milhaud was present to hear a piece of his on this same program and he went home to lunch with Ives. His possession of a

audience rioted, and a critic who heard the racket from outside, having arrived too late for the music, commented acidly: 'Initiative, Referendum — why not Recall?'

This concert was a milestone in the career of Ives's music because the two most influential American critics made a real attempt to understand the music. Lawrence Gilman, who had been bombarded for some years by that time with propaganda for the music of Ives from his friend Henry Bellamann, said of it: 'This music is as indubitably American in impulse and spiritual texture as the prose of Jonathan Edwards; and like the writing of that true artist and true mystic, it has at times an irresistible veracity and strength — an uncorrupted sincerity.' Olin Downes wrote about the music of 'Mr. St. Ives': 'There are ineptitudes, incongruities. The thing is an extraordinary hodgepodge, but something that lives and that vibrates with conviction is there. It is not possible to laugh this piece out of countenance . . . There is something in this music: real vitality, real naïveté and a superb self-respect . . . There is "kick" in the piece . . .'

Some of this was undoubtedly balm to Ives's soul, but on the other hand it was not for professional music critics that he had written his music, and the violent rejection of it by the majority of the hearers was again a shocking experience.

Henry Bellamann continued to write about Ives to the end of his life, and Schmitz carried Ives's name into his master classes in many American towns as well as to all the branches of his society (Pro Musica), but Schmitz came to feel, as he said himself, that a concert artist dared not

---

fine gold toothpick and his uninhibited use of it after lunch made a lasting impression on the New England household. Ives was pleased to have him tell Schmitz that he noticed in Ives's Fourth Symphony many things he had not yet seen in any other music.

identify himself with radically new music if he had his living to earn. Goossens was not attracted by Ives's music and made no attempt to explore it further nor to repeat the score he had learned — a matter of no surprise since even if he had come personally to care about the music, he could not then have played it without losing his orchestra. Since no demand for the music was created by this concert, nothing seemed to have happened so far as Ives could see; the friendly comments on the music did not efface the memory of the harsh or stupid ones, and he shrank from the knowledge that his name was associated with a major concert scandal.

Reinforcements, however, were coming up from another direction, and another period in the life of the music was about to begin. For the next ten or twelve years, the most active and determined friends of Ives's music were to be the experimental composers who were brought together by Henry Cowell's activities on behalf of twentieth-century music: John Becker, Wallingford Riegger, Carl Ruggles, Otto Luening and Nicolas Slonimsky, along with Cowell. These men were all writing music in ways very different from Ives and from each other, but they were all bent on experiment and on the exploration of fresh musical resources of various kinds, and they had all been subjected over many years to the same condescending laughter or violence of personal attack from performers and critics.

The generous welcome and unselfish support given by this little group to all kinds of new ideas in music was the kind of thing Ives believed in. These same qualities were to attract younger men in the 'thirties and 'forties — Bernard Herrmann, Lehman Engel, Jerome Moross, Gerald Strang, Ray Green, Lou Harrison, Frank Wigglesworth and Vladimir Ussachevsky — so that there has been a rare continuity and consistency in the activities of the *New Music* composers, who have all felt that a blow struck for Ives's music was a blow in favor of their own convictions.

When the quarterly *New Music* was launched in 1927, the 8000 personal notes scribbled on the backs of the circulars that the editor sent out during the summer brought in about 700 subscriptions at two dollars each; two came from Charles Ives. When the subscribers saw the first issue (*Men and Mountains* by Carl Ruggles), about half of the subscriptions were canceled. Ives, on the other hand, sent a check for twenty-five more subscriptions at once. The editor called on Ives to thank him, with a certain curiosity to meet the man whose music had so scandalous a reputation.

Face to face with Ives it was impossible not to feel his great personal force and integrity, nor to doubt his intelligence. Upon examination of some of Ives's scores, it was apparent that this was just the kind of music, — experimental, non-commercial — that *New Music* had been founded to disseminate. A request to print some of it met with some delay while Ives assured himself that the periodical was equally non-commercial and experimental. When he found that it was actually, as represented, a nonprofit undertaking that was financed when necessary by the editor, and that there was no money at all back of the venture, Ives decided to permit some of his scores to appear, with the unique proviso that the publisher was not to meet any of the expenses of production. This Ives insisted upon doing himself, for he wished, he said, not to be 'beholden' to any publishing house, even a non-profit one. *New Music,* of course, had expected to pay all costs, as any reputable publisher does, but under the circumstances Ives's generous condition was accepted as a gift to the enterprise.

The first Ives piece undertaken by *New Music* was the

second movement of the Fourth Symphony. It entailed absolutely unprecedented engraving problems, since there are sometimes as many as seventeen different rhythms going on at once. The engraver, Herman Langinger of the Golden West Music Press, in Los Angeles, studied the theory of modern music with *New Music*'s editor during the year the work was in preparation, in order to equip himself to solve the difficulties that faced him. No other engraver could possibly have dealt with the music satisfactorily at that time. The work finally appeared in January 1929, the first composition of Ives to be published rather than privately printed.*

When he and Ives first met late in 1927, Henry Cowell was on the way to Europe for his third concert and lecture tour. Recognizing in Ives's early scores musical materials and usages that had meanwhile made the reputation of men such as Milhaud, Hindemith, Stravinsky, and Schoenberg, along with a great deal that no one else had yet thought of, Cowell immediately began to include Ives's name among the really important creative figures of the early twentieth century, and to write and lecture about him persistently both abroad and at home.

Not long afterward he brought flint and tinder together when he introduced Ives and Nicolas Slonimsky; the resulting explosion had lasting consequences. Slonimsky, a prodigious musical personality, himself a composer, is a

* Ives's first publisher was the non-profit New Music Edition in the sense that its editor was the first to approach Ives unsolicited. But as with all of Ives 'firsts' some qualification is necessary here. One of the several lists of his compositions provided by Ives mentions an *Intercollegiate March* published by Pepper & Co., in Philadelphia in 1895. Some lists omit this; Ives himself is vague about it; and Pepper & Co. write (May 1951) that they have no record of such a publication. It seems likely that this was an ephemeral publication arranged by a friend without Ives's previous knowledge, either as a joke or a compliment.

man of extraordinary energy who was looking for new walls to scale. He was founder-conductor of the Chamber Orchestra of Boston and before the end of 1930 the group had given, in Boston, the first performance of Ives's *Three Places in New England*. Slonimsky repeated it on his New York program at Town Hall on 10 January 1931. The three American pieces played that day were heartily booed and hissed. It seems to have been during the performance of Carl Ruggles' *Men and Mountains* on this program that Ives suddenly stood up during the music and shouted at an uproarious auditor: 'Stop being such a God-damned sissy! Why can't you stand up before fine strong music like this and use your ears like a man!' Not all Slonimsky's skill could make up for the players' inability to understand all the demands of the music and the conductor has said himself that the performance was 'somewhat scrambling.' But there was good will in the effort and Ives told the conductor approvingly: 'Just like a town meeting — every man for himself. Wonderful how it came out!'

Undaunted by the antagonism and hilarity produced by such music, Slonimsky stubbornly played the *Three Places in New England* again when he was invited to appear as guest conductor with the Los Angeles Philharmonic Orchestra in December 1932. He was personally a great success as a conductor, but the uproar created by the music was still remembered disapprovingly by some of the orchestra's patrons fifteen years later. It was a reckless squandering of his future if he really wanted the position as conductor of one of the big orchestras which it seemed at that time he might easily have had. On this same trip to California Slonimsky played Ives's *Decoration Day* music at a New Music Society concert in San Francisco. He had already taken a program of music by North Americans to Cuba, where he led the Havana Philharmonic on 18 March 1931.

This had again included *Three Places in New England*, which generated a great enthusiasm for Ives in the regular conductor, the composer Amadeo Roldán, with the result that there were several later performances in Cuba.

Meanwhile, Henry Cowell had gone to Europe again, giving piano recitals of his own music and lecturing about American music generally, and the interest generated among avant-garde musicians and artists was such that he conceived the idea of a series of concerts to introduce orchestra works by experimental American composers. These were to be performed by several important European orchestras, and sponsored by the Pan-American Association of Composers. The fantastic devaluation of European currencies in the early 'thirties made everyone in Europe eager for American dollars, and it was partly sympathy with poverty-stricken European orchestra players that suggested to Cowell that he might find a way to channel some dollars in their direction if they would play some of the new American music. The general attitude of the orchestra managers whom he approached was that desirable as dollars might be, the playing of such music was almost too much to expect; but eventually they reluctantly agreed.

Ives was fired with enthusiasm for this project and offered part of the funds for it, enabling it to get started. When further support proved impossible to obtain, Ives undertook to meet all the expenses, although this necessitated increased domestic economy in a household where living standards were always plain, in order to avoid dipping into the capital of his music fund. Ives's health made it impossible for him to do any of the work connected with promoting the music he believed in, so he considered the contribution of the necessary money to be his 'share.'

The European concerts took place in 1931 and 1932. Slonimsky, who had enlarged his repertoire of Ives pieces to include three movements of *Holidays* (the *Fourth of July*, which is perhaps the toughest music ever mastered by a conductor, *Washington's Birthday*, and *Decoration Day*), conducted in Paris, Budapest, and Berlin, Anton Webern in Vienna, and Pedro Sanjuan in Madrid, always with one of the major symphony orchestras. The concerts created great excitement: laughter, protest, enthusiasm. Ives's music never occupied more than a single modest spot on each pair of programs, but several important critics singled it out for serious and admiring comment: 'Imagination and a strange genius . . . turbulent life of America . . .' 'The impressionistic lament of the twilight of the North American Indian . . .' 'Adorable freshness [Paris] . . .' 'Un véritable précurseur — un talent audacieux . . .' 'Truly national . . .' 'A strong, high, moving sentiment, free from the banalities of better-known works . . .' 'Ives is not imitative; he has something to say. He is a musical artist-painter, if such an expression may be used, an impressionist not without a mixture of naïve realism; his art is at times awkward and raw, but in him there is real power and true invention, thematically and rhythmically speaking, which does not follow either the fashion or authorities. Ives is, perhaps, the only one among the American composers whose art is truly national — in this he has something in common with Walt Whitman.'

The center of influence on American musical life had moved from Germany to France after the First World War, but the situation remained the same: most Americans went abroad to learn how to write or to play as well as Europeans did. So long as they presented themselves as students they were treated with condescension, molded carefully in well-established molds, and eventually reproached for developing the imitative skills that were all their teachers allowed them.

Paradoxically enough the only Americans really to be taken seriously by intelligent European musicians were those who made music without reference to European techniques. Vincent d'Indy had once remarked to Henry Bellamann that it was too bad that Americans did not 'inspire themselves from their own landscape and legends.' The reaction to the Pan-American Association concerts made it evident that there was a group of musicians and critics abroad — outside of conventional academic circles — who were looking for indications that composers in the United States had stopped imitating Europeans and were achieving something authentically their own. Professional musical life in the United States was still so sensitive to European opinion that no one could hope to make a career here who had not first received the stamp of critical approval in Paris, Berlin, and Vienna. It was the respectful and often admiring hearing given Ives's music by a few critics abroad that began in the early 1930's to suggest that the music of Ives was perhaps not the joke most musicians in America had at first supposed.

The first program in the United States that did not arouse as much cat-calling as it did applause took place at Yaddo, when on a program arranged by Aaron Copland seven of Ives's songs were sung by Hubert Linscott with Copland at the piano; the audience was an invited one and the songs were given a good deal of critical notice, most of it friendly.

At the Town Hall concert in 1931 the music had made an important friend in Paul Rosenfeld, who shared the increasing curiosity about where and what 'American' music was, and who found he liked Ives's *Three Places in New England*. Rosenfeld was something new in music critics, for he was willing to risk the critic's traditional reputation for professional detachment by inquiring of composers themselves what they thought they were doing. His articles in the *New Republic* and his books were of immense influence in creating a friendlier attitude toward the music of Americans, and the career of Ives's music was to benefit both directly and indirectly from this change. Arthur Berger was a younger critic in New York who, being a composer himself, was not afraid of being seen with other composers and who wrote that 'history is being made in our midst' in 1932.

As the European interest made itself felt in New York, it lent Ives's music an aura of comparative respectability which it had not enjoyed before. Ives's detachment from the professional musical scene turned him rapidly into a legend, so that it was not uncommon in the mid-'thirties to hear the music talked of enthusiastically by people who proved never to have heard any of it nor to have seen a score. Meanwhile Ives's music appeared on programs of the New Music Society on the Pacific Coast and of the composers' forums initiated during 1930–31 at the New School in New York. In 1933 two publications, an article in *Musical Quarterly* by Henry Bellamann and the symposium *American Composers on American Music* (with an article by Ives on music and another by Cowell on Ives) carried Ives's name and his ideas out among college students and teachers.

The year 1934 saw the first recording of an Ives work, when Nicolas Slonimsky played the *Barn Dance* from the music for *Washington's Birthday* (in the Symphony *Holidays*), and *In the Night* from the *Theatre Orchestra Set* with the Pan-American Orchestra, for *New Music Quarterly Recordings*. The same year Radiana Pazmor, accompanied by Genevieve Pitot, recorded one of the sturdiest and most impressive songs: *General Booth Enters Heaven* — also for *NMQR*. The *Seven Songs* were published by Cos Cob (later Arrow) Press, at the instigation of Aaron Copland, who wrote an article for *Modern Music* on Ives's songs. In 1935 Birchard in Boston made the first commercial venture with Ives's music when they published *Three Places in New England*. The first radio performance of an orchestra piece by Ives came also in the early 'thirties, when Bernard Herrmann played his own arrangement of the *Fugue* from Ives's Fourth Symphony with the CBS Orchestra. In 1937 another young composer, Lehman Engel, led his Madrigal Singers in Ives's setting of the *67th Psalm*. This was recorded by Columbia, the first recording by a major company.

Meanwhile the composer-conductor John Becker was active on behalf of contemporary music in the Great Lakes states, conducting, lecturing, and teaching, arousing curiosity, excitement, and contention over new music wherever he went; he deciphered and played some pieces of Ives for orchestra in the mid-'thirties.

News of other performances around the country and requests from a few enterprising people for copies of the music began to disturb the calm of the Ives household in a gratifying way, but on the whole this was a period when the interest and support of other composers were responsible for circulating the music: if it was heard it was because other composers arranged for the hearing. Ives's audience had grown, but it was still made up largely of supporters or explorers of the small avant-garde movements in the arts in the United States.

However, another champion, of a somewhat different line of descent, was quietly at work preparing an event that was to break down resistance to Ives's ideas in a major area of musical activity. The American pianist John Kirkpatrick had seen the score of the *Concord Sonata* in Paris in 1927 and had then thought it the maddest music imaginable. When in the early 1930's he finally determined to take possession of this rugged music if he could, he devoted years to preparing it, going over it with Ives, arranging some changes, setting it aside and returning doggedly to it. The result was a performance of a major Ives work that again created a riot in Town Hall (20 January 1939) — a riot of enthusiasm this time. It seems reasonably safe to say that this was the first performance of the whole work in New York.*

The audience responded so warmly that one movement had to be repeated, and on 24 February, at a second Town Hall program that was devoted entirely to Ives, Mr. Kirkpatrick repeated the whole Sonata by popular request. For the first time Ives's music generated the live response from an entire audience that its composer dreamed of. He had got across to the Majority Mind.

Ives himself, however, was not present. Kirkpatrick had played the Sonata for him privately, but on the night of

* The earliest performance set off by Ives's private distribution of the *Concord Sonata* and the *Essays* seems to have been the one that was arranged by Henry Bellamann, when Miss Lenore Purcell played it in New Orleans, October 1920. Robert Schmitz played part of it in Paris about 1925. On 1 May 1928, Ives's old friend Oscar Ziegler played the Alcott movement before the New York Historical Society, and on 14 November 1928, Anton Rovinsky included the Hawthorne movement on his Town Hall program. On 5 March of the same year, Katherine Heyman, giving the first broadcast in English for the Sorbonne Station of the Radio Institute of Paris, had included the Emerson movement; this seems to be the earliest broadcast of Ives's music. Arthur Hardcastle of Los Altos played part of the Sonata for lectures by Henry Cowell in the San Francisco Bay region about 1929. John Kirkpatrick gave a private performance of the whole sonata in Cos Cob, Connecticut, immediately before his Town Hall concert in 1939. In June 1939, Frances Mullen played the Emerson movement at one of the Evenings on the Roof in Los Angeles.

the concert Ives stayed at home. Kirkpatrick went off triumphantly to play the Sonata around the country, in Denver, Washington, and other places, while reviews and letters began to come to Ives, surprising him by the understanding and pleasure in the music expressed by a wide variety of people. Lawrence Gilman wrote: 'The greatest music composed by an American . . . music of breadth . . . profoundly stirring in its intensity and nobility of expression . . . astounding ability to fluctuate, combine and invent rhythms . . . A very large figure looms . . .' and of Kirkpatrick: 'an unobtrusive minister of genius.'

After the second concert Downes reported: 'Literati and cognoscenti were present in this knowing audience . . . If snobbism was present it was not the fault of a ruggedly individual composer. Articles acclaiming the sonata . . . recounting the strange career . . . had prepared the public for a sensation. Therefore many people who would have passed by the *Concord Sonata* before it had received critical approval without the flicker of an eyelash, were now present audibly and visually to be counted among those who really understood and appreciated the singular music of Mr. Ives.'

Kirkpatrick recorded the *Concord Sonata* for Columbia soon after the New York performances, but it didn't appear for several years. When it was finally issued in 1945, to everyone's astonishment its sales led the list of best-selling concert music for some months. The critical approval given the music when Kirkpatrick performed it generated a wave of interest among performers, who began to feel they might risk less than they had supposed in singing or playing Ives's music in public. Soon after the Kirkpatrick performance, Joseph Szigeti lent the Fourth Violin Sonata his powerful support in concert and recording, and both pianists and violinists began to feel the challenge, as singers had earlier, to show that they, too, could cope with music that might be difficult but that was clearly their own. In the 'thirties composers were the chief support of Ives's music, but the 'forties were to mark its circulation among performers of all kinds, and with this type of more conventional support went a sudden great expansion of the music's audience. The volumes of photostat copies of his chamber music that Ives had had bound and deposited in a few places were all at once in great demand, and there was a flurry of editing for publishers by the little group of fellow composers, now augmented by Lou Harrison, who had learned to puzzle out the manuscripts.

The season 1944–5 was the 70th anniversary year for both Ives and Schoenberg, and the fullest hearing Ives's music had yet had was at the Evenings on the Roof in Los Angeles, where on a series of programs devoted to the two septuagenarians all the available chamber music and several of the most daring songs were given.*

At the Second Annual Festival of Contemporary American Music sponsored by the Ditson Fund at Columbia University, one program was devoted to the chamber music of Charles Ives; Koussevitsky and Mitropoulos were in the audience. In the same year, 1946, he was elected to the National Institute of Arts and Letters, which is the greatest honor accorded any creative American (except for the

---

* After the death of Arnold Schoenberg in 1951, his widow mailed to Mr. and Mrs. Ives a sheet she found among his papers on which he had written the following:

> There is a great Man living in this Country — a composer.
> He has solved the problem how to preserve one's self and to learn.
> He responds to negligence by contempt.
> He is not forced to accept praise or blame.
> His name is Ives.

ultimate canonization that consists of election from the Institute to the smaller roster of the American Academy).

The next milestone had lasting reverberations, for when the composer Lou Harrison conducted the Third Symphony on a program of Barone's New York Little Symphony Orchestra in 1947, it was awarded the Pulitzer Prize. With his usual attempt at gruffness, Ives told the members of the Pulitzer Committee who made the award: 'Prizes are for boys. I'm grown up.' The story of 'the grand old man of American music' who had lived to win this famous prize twenty years after he last wrote any music, with a piece written roughly twenty years before that, broke into the news all over the country. Ives was glad the music was liked, but he was unimpressed by all the to-do and he refused all requests from metropolitan and news-service reporters for interviews and pictures. Finally he allowed a reporter from the local paper to come with a photographer. He was quoted as saying testily that 'prizes are the badges of mediocrity'; he gave the five hundred dollars away.

In 1948 the Boston Symphony, under Richard Burgin, gave the second Boston and New York performances of *Three Places in New England* — seventeen years after the first ones. Again Ives stayed home, but the letters from old friends who heard the music surprised and pleased him, and there were reminiscent notes about Ives in various Yale publications and in the insurance journals. A critic recalled his description of the piece after Slonimsky played it in Boston in 1931: he had called the first and third movements 'indistinguishable and interchangeable.' 'That was a foolish remark,' said he candidly in 1948 — an honest confession that cheered Ives by its integrity. The same year, Robert Shaw and the Collegiate Chorale gave an enthusiastic and highly successful performance of the *67th Psalm* and the *Harvest Home Chorales* in Carnegie Hall. A letter from Robert Russell Bennett about this time surprised Ives with word that the National Association for American Composers and Conductors had awarded him a medal for 'outstanding services to American music.'

By 1950, Kirkpatrick, Masselos, the Walden and New Music Quartets, and Joseph Szigeti had played major Ives works the country over. No college course or club program of contemporary music would now omit Ives, and American-born conductors, notably Dean Dixon, have played some of the orchestra pieces with symphonies abroad, in Vienna, Naples, Budapest, Amsterdam. It is only on American orchestra programs that it is not yet taken for granted that the music of Ives will appear regularly to represent America. Even after all the stir created by the honors awarded Ives the year before, critics were still complaining in 1947 that Ives was more written about than performed, that their knowledge of the big works was incomplete, that performances were still scant and sporadic. Yet he was widely accepted as 'a fundamental expression of America . . . who may be the decisive inspiration for a new generation . . . one of the most vital and creative figures of this century.'

It is only fair to say that the delay in performing Ives's orchestra music can no longer be blamed on musicians, critics, and concert-goers. In spite of the great audience and critical success of the only two major orchestra performances the music has had in this country since the 1930's (the Boston Symphony program in 1948 and the first performance of the Second Symphony by the New York Philharmonic under Bernstein in 1951), there is at the moment of writing a serious hurdle ahead of the music — one that faces not only the music of Ives but all music of an idiom later than the romantic nineteenth century. This is the hurdle into the regular symphonic repertory, so that the big works can be heard often and well played, and can become at least as familiar as the *Pines of Rome* or the *Heldenleben*.

Part of the difficulty has been that Ives not only calls for unusual instrumental combinations, but that he aggravates the situation by presenting problems in performance that require additional rehearsals at enormous expense. He is not alone in this, although his music presents a rather extreme example of it. The more responsible conductors, who insist on a hearing for contemporary works, have tacitly agreed with orchestra managers on a quota system: the 'difficult' works they may introduce are limited to two, three, or four a year. Until the mid-'forties no American conductor who by training and experience knew his own cultural tradition could get a job with a major symphony orchestra, so almost all the 'difficult' works chosen by the conductors of the major orchestras have not unnaturally been European ones.

The demands of the Musicians' Union, which quite rightly insists on a living wage and a full season's work for its men, have had the unintended effect of crystallizing the personnel of the symphony orchestra to suit the requirements of the works most popular at the time the union contracts were first put into effect — the works of the popular nineteenth-century big-noise composers: Wagner, Tchaikovsky, Strauss, and so on. Orchestras find it so nearly impossible to make ends meet financially that demands for 'irregular' extra men — saxophone players, a fourth flute player, a fourth trumpet, a second pianist, or extra drummers (most of them incursions into symphonic sound from the dance and theater orchestras and bands of Ives's youth) are a real threat to the budget. If a composer varies his instrumentation by keeping some of the men on the stage idle temporarily, to the management it not unnaturally seems wasteful, since those men have to be paid for a full evening's work anyway. Moreover, it is always the familiar works that fill the hall safely and surely. So managerial pressure will always be on the side of well-established kinds of music — which have the added virtue of being so familiar to the players that they require a minimum of rehearsal time.

The impasse is a serious one, but there are forces at work on it, and the situation that now makes twentieth-century music less often played than audiences and performers would like may well change before long. When it does, admirers of Ives's music will be the first to benefit, for the interest in it and response to it now displayed by American conductors and American audiences are real.

VIII

After Retirement

———

In 1929, the year before Charles Ives finally retired formally from business, the amount of insurance issued by Ives & Myrick was more than $49,000,000. Had he wished, the senior member of such a firm, which was by that time the largest of its kind in the country, could have retired many times a millionaire. This Ives declined to do, for contact with astronomical amounts of money had never succeeded in making him feel right about reserving to himself more than what his calculations had shown him to be his reasonable share of the country's wealth. His whole attitude toward money has been original and consistent. He never drew from the business more than was needed to keep his family comfortable in their unostentatious way, and he provided against illness and retirement by means of an annuity. He also set aside a moderate fund, the income from which was intended to meet the expense of copying or printing or performing his music. He has never been averse to letting his music be known, but he has wished always to meet all expenses connected with its circulation himself. The sums spent on his own music have normally been matched by contributions toward the support of other contemporary music, channeled as a rule through those organizations that he felt sure were devoting themselves to the strongest new music.

His contributions to contemporary music are the expression of a sense of social responsibility, but they come also from a very personal desire to spare other less fortunate composers some of the inevitable burdens of an expensive and financially unrewarding profession. The League of Composers, the International Society for Contemporary Music, and Arrow Press, along with New Music (to mention only organizations still active today) have each received a substantial sum — in small amounts at a time — over a period of years. The organizations that attracted his special attention were all small and young and more or less penniless, and Ives recognized that they risked complete financial disaster by promoting the dissonant and new.

One of the main objectives of the periodical *New Music* was its circulation, by means of a nearly world-wide free list, among composers and the small experimental music groups who might be expected to study the scores and understand them. Ives had been pleasantly surprised to receive comments from various unexpected quarters on the first score of his that *New Music* printed. So when in 1930 the editor asked for more scores to print, he agreed.

He first made two unusual conditions, however. He wished not only to pay the costs of production of his own music, as before, but he asked to be allowed to contribute an equal amount to the publication of important but non-commercial works by other people. He refused all editorial responsibility: *New Music* was to go on exactly as it was; but any publication of music of his was to be matched by that of somebody else. This encouragement to the periodical came at a vital moment, when the original subscribers had been much reduced by shock at the music that appeared, and the people for whom it was really designed had not yet responded in numbers sufficient to carry it. For two or three years Ives took care of the difference between the subscriptions and the quarterly printing bill, and the editor financed advertising and mailing costs. Then subscriptions and individual sales began to rise again, and Ives settled down to a steady contribution of fifty dollars a month — about a third of the annual printing expense. This dependable backing, small though it sounds, has been crucial for an enterprise that runs on a shoestring, because it insured an independent and broadly inclusive editorial policy.

Ives's second condition for further publication was attached to a complaint. It seems he had been incensed to find that, according to its custom, *New Music* had taken out a copyright in the composer's name for the part of his Fourth Symphony that it had issued. Ives stalked up and down the room, growing red in the face to an alarming degree and flailing the air with his cane: 'EVERYBODY who wants a copy is to have one! If anyone wants to copy or reprint these pieces, that's FINE! This music is not to make money but to be known and heard. Why should I interfere with its life by hanging on to some sort of personal legal right in it?'

Much later, about 1945, Harold Spivacke, chief of the

music division of the Library of Congress, addressed a discreet and kindly note to *New Music*'s editor, pointing out that the periodical had made a grievous and damaging mistake. Dr. Spivacke's attention had just been called to the fact that the editor had forgotten to copyright any of the works by Charles Ives that it had printed. A consultation was suggested, to see if there might not be some way of repairing the error. The consultation was held and Ives's point of view explained, but it was apparent that Dr. Spivacke never could quite bring himself to believe in the existence of a composer who objected to reserving his own rights in his music.

Although rising costs and lowered interest rates have greatly reduced Ives's fund for music, his fear of being influenced by outside demands and ideas for his music made him adamant about meeting all its expenses himself for so many years that it has been difficult to convince him that times have changed and that commercial publishers are now willing to take this responsibility. When the big publishing houses first began to want a work of his in their catalogues, Ives got a great deal of fun out of his letter of authorization: the first page gave permission to publish the work on two conditions, the first of which was that no money should go to the composer, as he did not wish to make any money from his music. This was of course pleasant hearing to publishers, who are inclined to feel that theirs is the major contribution to any published piece of music. But overleaf came the second condition: the publisher was not to make a profit on the publication either, and free copies were always to be available to anyone who asked for one. For some time negotiations ended at that point.

After 1946 there was such a multiplication of activity with Ives's music that he could no longer cope with the correspondence and general bother entailed, and he found commercial publishers more useful in these respects than he expected. So he resigned himself to the more usual contractual arrangements, the more readily as it occurred to him that if publishers were determined to pay royalties on his music, Ives could assign any sums due him to somebody else. This he has done consistently, usually in return for work done by another composer in preparing the work for performance or publication. Once or twice a check for royalties or performance rights has been sent to Ives by mistake, and he has mailed it right back with some indignation.

As the life of Ives's music gathered momentum in the 'thirties and 'forties, the life of its composer declined toward a calm more apparent than real, for he is as full of passionate devotion to the things he believes in, and as concerned over their successes and failures, as he ever was. Since 1927 the consideration that has governed every detail of the lives of both Charles Ives and his wife has been his threatening health: heart disease, diabetes and cataracts (over both eyes, inoperable because of the heart condition) all limit the day's activities in varying degrees. Mrs. Ives's great concern has been to maintain a quiet atmosphere and an inner serenity that will keep all pressure and excitement, with their real danger to her husband's health, at a distance. Her calm demeanor is a notable achievement. She once mentioned a letter from the insistent head of a musical organization who urged her to phone him at once, 'on urgent business.' This struck Mrs. Ives as funny: 'What have I to do with "urgent business?" ' she inquired. Walden Pond might have been just outside the windows on East 74th Street.

Mr. and Mrs. Ives both follow contemporary events, but at a slight remove from the immediacy of radio broadcasts:

Mr. Ives naturally prefers the weekly and monthly summaries of news as being less polemical, and he owns no radio. He watches eagerly, when he is able, for indications of improvement in the aspects of human affairs that he has most at heart: international relations and the outlawing of war, above all, and the position of minority groups, and human independence all over the world. And, in the musical world, for indications that people are giving up their 'mollycoddle ways with music easy on the ears' in favor of 'the hard way up the mountain.' A naturally sociable person, he would often enjoy more visitors than his health will allow, and it is sometimes difficult for Mrs. Ives to decide whether the excitement of discussion is worse for him than the lack of an opportunity to communicate his indignation or pleasure.

When he is well enough he settles down every day after breakfast to go through *The New York Times* almost from beginning to end, and he has read the London *Spectator* regularly for many years. But there are long periods when he is not able to stand the agitation that the crabwise progress of the human race toward peace and perfection creates in him. An almost incoherent spot in one of his music manuscripts contains several incomplete pages of libelous fury at Hearst and yellow journalism generally, of a violence that a man with a long history of heart disease cannot afford.

Because his highly susceptible nervous system reacts in various unfortunate ways to any surprise or stress, he sees only old friends; he has been obliged for many years to avoid meeting strangers. The session that produced Smith's fine portrait for *Life* put its subject to bed for three weeks, in spite of the fact that Ives had agreed to it in advance and reported that he liked the photographer. Once or twice unknown admirers have penetrated his retirement uninvited; at least one of these was badly frightened by the excitable flow of paradox and incomprehensible punning that came his way in a flood, unaware that this was only an unusually animated form of the screen that Ives has customarily held up between the world and his personal thought. He gave up his daily neighborhood walks in New York for a while, after strangers had once or twice recognized him and stopped him on the street. He is not inordinately shy, for he was never averse, as a younger man, to speaking out in public when he felt his opinion had a right to be heard. He occasionally consented to give a speech at a convention or a dinner of insurance men when he was still active in business, and on his first trip abroad in 1924 he approached dozens of strangers in several countries to get their opinions about bringing wars to an end. But he has to a great degree the dignified New Englander's determination to separate his work in the world, his public career, from his personal life; moreover, anything to do with his music sets up a special strain. To be revered, or even admired, at this late date, strikes him as silly after all he has been through as a composer — much as he would naturally like to believe it real and deserved.

For many years Mr. and Mrs. Ives have spent the summer in the wooded hills of Connecticut, on their West Redding farm, usually alone with Carrie, the maid, and, until her death at an incredible age, Christofina the cat. The house is dark, cool, and spacious, and full of books, with a great window looking north over rolling meadows to a little pond frequented by small friendly wild animals. A noisy wren has nested undisturbed for many years just over the front door. Beyond the immediate hills are the Berkshires — a view Mr. Ives seems never to tire of contemplating. When he is able he likes to walk out into the woods behind the house and sit alone quietly on a stump listening to the woodland sounds of summer. Or he may go off to chat over the stone wall with one of the neighboring farmers. There is a cheerful relaxed period after supper when Mr. Ives helps Carrie with the dishes. Time was when he enjoyed haying and doing chores around the place, but it is a good many years since he has been allowed the strenuous physical activity he used to love.

In the winter the Iveses leave the country unwillingly to retreat to the old brownstone front they have occupied since 1925 in New York; there, too, they live very quietly. Mrs. Ives reads aloud a great deal — poetry, philosophy, natural history — and occasionally an old friend may be summoned for a visit, on one of Ives's good days, to talk about music. In New York as in the country, Ives has a small music work room, piled with papers and manuscripts and containing a piano, apart from the family's living quarters. He has never lost his ability to give an acceptable demonstration of the complex rhythms in his orchestra scores, and he has never abandoned composition entirely, for on rare occasions he will add a few notes to his *Universe Symphony,* a work that he has planned from the beginning to leave unfinished.

He often feels very restless, and a visitor, who remembered how much he used to enjoy his brief jaunts in the United States and in Europe, once suggested a winter excursion to Florida. There was an immediate stamping of feet and waving of his cane across the room as Mr. Ives exploded to his feet: 'Florida!' he exclaimed indignantly, 'Florida is for sissies! Only sissies go to Florida!' This effectively closed the subject of winter travel. Our informant was reminded of the elderly New England lady who replied to her grandchildren's concern over her chilly house: 'My dears, no New Englander expects to be really comfortable in the winter.'

Ives has never bought a radio nor a record-player, partly because he felt no confidence in the quality of mechanically distributed music, but also because of a hearing disability that is not deafness but the result of a disarrangement of his nervous system that brings about a wavery distortion of sounds that is intensified when he tries to listen to music. He first noticed it about 1932, in London, at a concert where some music of Brahms was being played: the high pitches were suddenly tremulous and distorted.

His vision was affected in the same way, and so were his hands. He grew a beard rather than struggle with shaving, and his letters to friends during the 'thirties are full of profane apologies for his shaky writing. This blurring of visual and auditory images and the trembling of his hands is fortunately intermittent, but it is increased whenever he has tried to concentrate on music.

This is the reason why his wife and daughter, in the role of amanuensis, have written his letters for so many years, and why he has had to depend on various composer friends for readying his scores and sketches for performance and publication. Nicolas Slonimsky, John Becker, Bernard Herrmann, Lou Harrison, and Henry Cowell have all rendered Ives this service at intervals for many years. His indication of his intentions is usually definite and full, so an editor as a rule need not contribute much personally; the chief problem has been the illegibility of the pencil sketches, many of which lay in Ives's Connecticut barn untouched for thirty years. Copies or reconstructions derived from his complicated abbreviations and cross-references are always submitted to him for his approval; sometimes, however, the editing has had to be described to him note by note, when he was momentarily unable to see the scores.

The impression given several people, that no one else has ever quite so well understood the music nor done so much for it, stems less from a sense of historical accuracy than from the composer's wholehearted surprise and excitement at any welcome given the music. In the same way more than one man has got the impression that his is the only editorial help ever to be really satisfactory to Mr. Ives, because of the warmth with which any help is always acknowledged. As far as appreciation of trouble taken by one composer on behalf of another goes, the warmth is certainly sincere. It seems not to cover changes made to facilitate performance, however, even when these were agreed to at the time. Ives has occasionally consented, upon urgent representations from the conductor proposing to play a work, to allow certain simplifications; but he has invariably regretted this afterward as being an undesirable concession to ease and sloth. At least once he rose and stalked angrily from his seat in Town Hall during his own piece, although he seems to have listened to the end from the back of the hall. Another time he went to hear a group of his songs sung in New York by the most famous baritone of the day. When he saw the songs on the program, however, he exclaimed that they were the *easiest* things he'd written, and he got up indignantly before the music began and went home.

In recent years he has had to refuse to go over his music with performers and conductors because of his unstable nervous system, and this explains in part his failure to sense the great progress his music has made toward general understanding and acceptance. He seems to be unable to feel any confidence in a prospective performance; it is as if he were still bracing himself in the old way against disappointment, unable to realize that such necessity is past. Although his music is increasingly understood and liked and usually now performed extremely well, Ives has not lost the habit of incredulity, and the anticipation of a performance calls up frustrating memories and a sense of dread that must go back to the shock of reactions to the music more than thirty years ago. When the writers were describing to him the sympathetic performances and the warm response of the audience to his *Harvest Home Chorales* and the *67th Psalm,* when the Collegiate Chorale performed them under Robert Shaw in 1948, Ives was deeply moved. After a long silence he recovered himself and remarked, obviously out of a perusal of the uncomfortable past: 'Robert Shaw is not much like Frank Damrosch, is he!' — a conclusion with which we were able to agree. For a long time he showed no interest in hearing any of the recordings of his music, but when his daughter and her husband gave him a record-player one Christmas, he did eventually try to hear some of the pieces, with a certain amount of success and pleasure.*

Aside from the early church and band performances and fragmentary readings by friends or by small theater orchestra groups, Ives seems not to have heard more than one or two incomplete performances of his larger orchestra pieces before he abandoned any sustained creative work. In 1953 he declared that this fact has been much exaggerated, and that actually he did hear all four of his symphonies, except for the last movement of the Fourth, tried over for him by

* The first recording of an orchestra piece by Ives was made by Slonimsky for *New Music Quarterly Recordings* in 1934; this was the *Barn Dance* from *Washington's Birthday* and *In the Night* from the *Set for Theatre Orchestra. General Booth* was recorded by Radiana Pazmor for *NMQR* in the same year. The first recording by one of the major companies took place when Lehman Engel conducted the *67th Psalm* with his Madrigal Singers for Columbia, in 1936. After John Kirkpatrick recorded the *Concord Sonata* (No. 2 for pianoforte) for Columbia and Szigeti the Fourth Violin Sonata for *NMQR* and the League of Composers, recordings by smaller companies multiplied; they have been issued from Polymusic (Elaine Music Shop), Oceanic, Concert Hall Society, Hamline University, Artists' Records, Alco, Radio Station WCBM, Disc (Period Records), SPA and Yaddo Recordings; others are in preparation.

various theater orchestras at an hour when the audience was small — as for instance at the Globe Theatre, where the manager once came out and made the men resume the usual repertoire, saying their experiments were bad for business. These are all works written for a much larger orchestra, of course, but Ives felt the theater men 'got through the music fairly well' — much better than the groups of symphony players he occasionally paid to come to his house to see what they could make of one of his scores, and who required six or eight rehearsals and many cuts before they could make the *Washington's Birthday* music sound acceptable, for instance. This same piece was played by Stokowski with the CBS orchestra 21 February 1954, after a single rehearsal.

Ives went to the Franco-American Society concerts in 1925 and 1927, and he did hear one of the concerts conducted by Nicolas Slonimsky in New York, either in 1931 or 1934. He was not present at either of John Kirkpatrick's programs in 1939, when he might have sensed the favorable response and excitement of the whole hall, nor did he go to hear Szigeti play his Fourth Violin Sonata, nor the Boston Symphony and Collegiate Chorale concerts in 1948.

Ives was not in Europe when the Pan-American Association first presented his music there in 1931 and 1932, but a comment on the programs by Philip Hale in Boston aroused Ives's ire by its lack of logic, and the autobiographical notes seem to have been initiated when Ives set down several hundred indignant words in refutation — not for publication but 'for the record.'

An . . . inference given in the more or less sweeping statements of Hale's is that conductors of American orchestras do not like the music of modern American composers. [This] would imply that conductors had examined (and carefully enough to be able to play) the greater part of those composers' music.

I imagine that my own actual experience is true of some of the other composers: during the 20 years ending 1919, only one conductor had seen any of my music. One in 1910 did try over a part of a first symphony which I completed in college in 1898.*

In the thirty years ending in 1929, two other conductors saw one score,† and the same score, of mine; and another, Mr. Eugene Goossens, played one movement of the Fourth Symphony in 1927.

In spite of Ives's conscientious contributions to the groups that were presenting new kinds of music, he did not as a rule go to their concerts. In a letter written to E. Robert Schmitz in 1931, Ives declared he had up to that time neither heard nor seen any music of Schoenberg or of Hindemith. Elsewhere he says he first heard a piece by Stravinsky in 1919 or 1920. This was a part of *Firebird,*

> . . . and I thought it was morbid and monotonous; the idea of a phrase, usually a small one, was good enough, and interesting in itself, but he kept it going over and over and it got tiresome. It reminded me of something I had heard of Ravel, whose music is of a kind I cannot stand: weak, morbid and monotonous; pleasing enough, if you want to be pleased.

In 1923 or 1924 I also heard Stravinsky's *Rossignol*

---

* This was Walter Damrosch, as mentioned earlier. Dr. Damrosch asked to see Ives's Second Symphony, but neither played it nor returned the score. When the work was to be played by the New York Philharmonic in 1951, the score could not be found, and it had to be reconstituted from the earlier pencil score and then recopied, at great expense.

† One of these was Gustav Mahler, who told Ives he would play the Third Symphony in Europe. But Mahler died before this intention could be carried out, and this score, too, was lost.

> . . . I have never heard nor seen the score of the
> *Sacre du Printemps* . . . Putnam's Camp, supposed
> to be influenced by Stravinsky, was written long before
> Stravinsky's name was known . . . Personally, I do
> not think they have anything in common.

Ives also emphatically contradicted an assumption Hale
had made:

> All of the music that I have written, with the exception
> of twelve or fifteen songs, was completed before I had
> seen or heard any of the music of the European com-
> posers cited by Hale in Boston as influencing the
> American composers on Slonimsky's European pro-
> grams.
> It is interesting to hear that I am influenced by Hinde-
> mith, who did not start to compose until about 1920,
> several years after I had completed the music, good or
> bad, which Hale says is influenced by Hindemith!
> It happens that the music of mine referred to (*Three
> New England Places*) was completed almost a decade
> before Hindemith became a composer. Up to the
> present [late in 1931] I have not seen or heard any of
> Hindemith's music.

The general tendency among music critics of the time to
blame Stravinsky or Hindemith for anything in music they
didn't understand stimulated Ives to write further about
his music and its history, and to write down what he could
recall of the genesis of some of the pieces. This often
brought up the memory of painful frustrations as well, and
led to severe disquisitions on human limitations, especially
laziness before the unfamiliar, ignorance, even plain stu-
pidity, and similar undesirable human attributes. Such
writing was a healthy safety-valve for an un-understood
composer, although Ives was at the same time profoundly

convinced that such un-understanding was inevitable, and temporary, and could not cloud over a great work for-ever.

Another less personal aspect of his desire to establish the facts 'for the sake of the record,' has occupied Ives's mind between more or less severe bouts of illness for many years. He sees to it that all references in print to his music are carefully collected, and with his daughter's help he has had all such references typed out and bound, along with copies of fan letters, of articles published and unpublished, radio announcements, blurbs on record album covers, reviews, notes from concert programs, paragraphs copied from the Yale alumni magazine and various insurance trade journals, and so on. The 'grey books' are then loaned to people who want statements from Ives or information about his music. They include some, but not all, of the reviews that have most roused his indignation. He conceives of the volumes as being a record of 'the progress of the music toward understanding and the triumph of the Ideal.'

After figuring as one of Paul Rosenfeld's 'discoveries of a music critic' in 1932, Ives must find a certain monotony in the headlines over the years: 'Charles Ives Emerges'; 'Tardy Recognition'; ' "New" Genius: 72'; 'Chronological Phenomenon'; 'Charles Ives Is Rediscovered'; 'Belated Tom-Tom for Genius'; 'A Prophet with Honor'; 'Charles Ives at Last.' The printed programs show a clearer progress, for pieces that appeared for a long time only with other new kinds of music at concerts of the small avant-garde groups now jostle Beethoven and Debussy as a matter of course, and there are occasional all-Ives programs or pro-gram series in various parts of the country and over the air.

The Pulitzer award in 1947 touched off a series of dis-concerting experiences: among other things, a press as-sociation photographer was ejected from the West Redding kitchen, where he had penetrated unannounced, only to be kept at bay by a freshly painted pantry floor. The secretary of Ives's class circulated mimeographed postcards to the members of Yale '98 that began: 'Great Composer!' and concluded, with singular inappropriateness, 'Orchids to Ives!' A phrenologist wrote from Europe to request 'a head of Charles Ives' to study, and there has been an increasing barrage from all over the country by students who ask for the sort of detail that Hollywood stars are accustomed to provide, with blanks to be filled out about tastes, hobbies, and the 'inspiration' for his music. Ph.D. candidates write to ask that Ives contribute his complete analysis of his chamber works or his songs to their thesis, and a psychology student asked for an interview, as he was doing a thesis on musical personalities: he proposed to give Mr. Ives a Rorschach test. Shut-ins ask for autographed photographs for their collections, and music libraries request the gift of an autograph score. Ives recognizes well enough, in theory, that the man and his music are one, but he has little patience with the public mania for personal details and mementoes and pictures. To defeat it is one of his small private jokes: one rather dim and blurred snapshot has served him for most such requests, and he will send a *photostat* of a manuscript cheerfully enough.

The news magazines and the fashionable periodicals that record various kinds of established distinction by 1950 had all carried brief articles and photographs of Ives, and Southern Music Publishers set in motion a long-range project for most of his unpublished music. The discovery and rediscovery of Charles Ives and his music may now fairly be said to be at an end; it should not be necessary again. When Ives troubles to look around him he can be sure there is no danger that his name will be forgotten or his music disappear unheard.

In spite of his deeply rooted skepticism about the performance and reception of his music, Ives always said that if his Second Symphony were ever performed in Carnegie Hall, he would go to hear it, for it was full of nostalgic references to music of the period when his father was still alive, and he thought he could enjoy listening to it. To have his music played in the great concert hall that was associated with his early concert-going in New York, when he must have dreamed that music of his yet to be written would one day be heard there, was obviously something he had hoped for in his lifetime.

But in 1951 when Leonard Bernstein announced that he would conduct several performances of this work with the New York Philharmonic, Ives grew more and more upset at the idea of hearing it, although Bernstein even offered to set one of the rehearsals at any hour that would suit Mr. Ives, and to arrange for him to be quite alone and invisible in the darkened hall. Still Ives could not make up his mind to go.

Mrs. Ives went to the *première* without him and sat with her daughter and son-in-law, one of her brothers and his wife, and the writers, in a box near the stage. At the end of the performance Bernstein applauded the players and then turned toward the Ives box to join in the wild and prolonged applause that rose from the hall. Realizing that Mrs. Ives was not grasping its extent, a guest touched her arm to suggest she turn away from the stage to see the cheering, clapping audience below her, which rose in the distance to the remote galleries. The warmth and excitement suddenly reached her and she said in a heart-breaking tone of pure surprise: 'Why, they *like* it, don't they!'

The critics wrote warmly about the music: 'of unique inspiration and a noble elevation of thought,' said Olin Downes, and Virgil Thomson called the symphony 'unquestionably an authentic work of art.' Ives's family and friends repeatedly assured him that the work was beautifully played and that the audience really liked it. So when the piece was broadcast a week later Ives did venture downstairs to listen to it on the maid's little radio in the kitchen. He was so happy about the quality of the performance, which was far finer than anything he ever expected, that he emerged from the kitchen doing an awkward little jig of pleasure and vindication. This seems to have been the only unqualified pleasure in an orchestra performance that Ives has ever had.

Ives is in his eightieth year as this is written, but he cannot yet be said to have 'settled into serenity.' On the whole, however, his interest in the stir and bustle that accompany fame is slight, for he has always been preoccupied with larger concerns. In 1949, Howard Taubman of *The New York Times* was allowed to come for almost the only interview that Ives has ever given. He assured Ives that he had anticipated all the famous men of our day in their innovations and Ives put the subject in its place with a wave of the hand: 'That's not my fault,' he said.

The concluding lines of the *Essays Before a Sonata* express what Charles Ives feels to be the relation between life and music. Written in 1919, this is what he would still wish to say today to every thoughtful artist:

The intensity with which techniques and media are organized and used, tends to throw the mind away from a common sense and toward manner — and thus . . . the Byronic fallacy, that one who is full of turbid feelings *about himself* is qualified to be some sort of an artist . . . It may be that when a poet . . . becomes conscious that he is in the easy path of any particular idiom, that he is helplessly prejudiced in favor of any particular means of expression, that his manner can be classified as modern or classic . . . that [a musician's] interests lie in the French school or the German school — that he favors a contrapuntal groove, a sound-coloring one, a sensuous one, a successful one or a melodious one — in a word, when he becomes conscious that his style is his personal own — then it may be that the value of his substance is not growing, that he is trading an inspiration for a bad habit, and finally, that he is reaching fame, permanence or some other undervalue, and that he is getting farther and farther from a perfect truth.

But on the contrary side of the picture, if this poet, composer and laborer is open to all the overvalues within his reach, if he stands unprotected from all the showers of the absolute which may beat upon him — if he is willing to use or learn to use . . . any and all lessons of the infinite that humanity has received and thrown to man, that nature has exposed and sacrificed, that life and death have translated, if he accepts all and sympathizes with all, is influenced by all . . . *then* it may be that the value of his substance, its value to himself, to his art, to all art, even to the Common Soul, is growing, and approaching nearer and nearer to perfect truths — whatever they are and wherever they may be.

Part Two

___

MUSIC

IX

Ives's Use of Musical Materials

'A TERRIBLY HARD TASTE OF MUSIC'

For most people the really baffling aspect of Ives's music is the multiplicity of simultaneous events and ideas in it. In spite of appearances, this is never a helter-skelter piling up of irrelevant matter; on the contrary, there is always some quite clear concept involved that can be reduced to comprehensible terms, though not always without a little trouble. Particularly in the later, larger works, one is easily lost. Yet no matter how involved the use of musical materials may be, it is always possible to discover unifying factors, unfamiliar and unexpected as applied to music though these often are.

It is important to remember that just as Ives saw social problems, his business, and his personal life in the light of his Universalist philosophy, so he shaped his musical materials in accordance with that philosophy. In the *Essays* he gives the clue to this connection:

Nature loves analogy and abhors repetition and explanation. Unity is too generally conceived of, or too easily accepted, as analogous to form, and form as analogous to custom, and custom to habit.

He feels that music, like other truths, should never be immediately understood; there must always remain some further element yet to be disclosed. A complete musical statement, in all its clarity and simplicity, like any absolute truth, is an ultimate, not a beginning. Ives reserves it, therefore, for the culmination of a work.

Ives concerns himself first of all with the forms of nature and their mysterious and complex behavior, rather than with any mathematically symmetrical and balanced repetition and permutation; these he believes may lead to distortion. Even vagueness may be, at times, 'an indication of nearness to a perfect truth.'

He finds one principle of unity in the sonata, because it deals with the resolution of two contrasting themes. The two-sidedness of reality, all the paradoxes of existence, are present to all Ives's thinking. They often make his ideas difficult reading, his statements hard to follow, and his most casual conversation disconcerting. This is because he believes that full expression of the opposing aspects of any idea whatever is a necessary step on the way to perfect truth, since only in this way can the common basis for the integration of these opposites be found. Their contrasting facets will ultimately, he believes, be seen as different aspects of the same thing. Ives's interest is in this *process toward* integration; with Emerson he abhors the spiritual inactivity that comes from the conviction that one possesses the truth in its final form. He envisages a series of integrations of dualities, each of which as it is achieved is seen as a sort of partial or temporary truth, a truth which then becomes only one aspect of another set of opposites which sooner or later must be resolved in its turn. This struggle toward truth and integration is the nearest man can come to absolute truth, in Ives's view; but he feels the very effort required imparts a certain unity and coherence of its own.

Therefore to think hard, and say what is thought, regardless of consequences, is a man's obligation. Comfort, repose, sloth, easy acceptance of the obvious or the customary are the great sins in Ives's lexicon.

To achieve beauty in accordance with accepted standards does not interest Ives, because he believes that people's notions of beauty depend upon what they are used to, or whatever will bother them least. 'Beauty in music is too often confused with something that lets the ears lie back in an easy chair.' Ives prefers to put his hearers' ears to work, and he points out that the ear can take in much more than it is used to if it must. To concern one's self with beauty primarily is to risk 'pretty music,' or 'nice music,' or mere sensuous beauty, or some other superficiality that diverts one from the search for spiritual strength and integrity. Besides, 'dissonances,' he says, 'are becoming beautiful.'

Nor does Ives create a work of art for the sake of expressing himself. He has no patience with those who believe themselves qualified as composers because they are 'full of turbid feeling about themselves — the Byronic fallacy.' 'The nearer we get to the mere expression of emotion, the further we get away from art . . . Should not the intellect have some part?'

Ives is often supposed devoted to program music because of the anecdotal nature of his own accounts of his music. Actually, it never follows stories nor imitates sounds literally for more than a moment. These extra-musical ideas are rather a jumping-off place, an observation point for the behavior of things in the universe. For Ives the meaning of an event seems to lie in the behavior of the elements that create it, and when he wants to convey an emotion about something, he reproduces the behavior of the sounds that are associated with it, their approach and departure, their pace and drive, interweaving and crossing — all this by analogy, which seems to be the way he approaches reality, rather than by description or literal imitation. He puts the wedge formation of a football team onto score paper to see how it would sound as music, for instance. Often he does reproduce several aspects of reality as he first observed them, but from their behavior he establishes the musical treatment, carrying the ideas gained from this kind of observation forward to make a system of musical behavior out of something first perceived on a quite different level.

Examples may make this clearer. The germ of Ives's complicated concept of polyphony seems to lie in an experience he had as a boy, when his father invited a neighboring band to parade with its team at a baseball game in Danbury, while at the same time the local band made its appearance in support of the Danbury team. The parade was arranged to pass along the main street as usual, but the two bands started at opposite ends of town and were assigned pieces in different meters and keys. As they approached each other the dissonances were acute, and each man played louder and louder so that his rivals would not put him off. A few players wavered, but both bands held together and got past each other successfully, the sounds of their cheerful discord fading out in the distance. Ives has reproduced this collision of musical events in several ways: From it, for example, he developed the idea of combining groups of players (sections of the orchestra) to create simultaneous masses of sound that move in different rhythms, meters, and keys. Thus his polytonality may be polyharmonic, each harmonic unit being treated like a single contrapuntal voice (as the bands played two separate tunes, each with its own harmonic setting); and it may also be polyrhythmic.

Again, Ives was impressed and moved, as a boy, by the magnificent outpourings at camp meetings, when several hundred people, many of them quite tuneless in the ordinary sense, sang 'praises unto the Lord' with their whole hearts. He felt that all the sounds had a certain consistency of behavior and so, instead of reproducing the single melody line that was the technical intention, he reproduced what actually went on. He has several times surrounded a plain melody with a wide band of tones, sounding faintly all the pitches close to the tone of theoretical musical intention. This reproduces the intense effect of mass singing in which some people sharpen the pitch involuntarily, while the stolid temperaments never do get up to the actual pitch of the tune at all. This technique produces chords in groups of seconds, which he then occasionally uses in other ways, free of any extra-musical connection. The same idea had occurred to him earlier, when he tried to reproduce the sounds of the drum on the piano. Triads wouldn't do it properly, but small clusters of adjacent tones suited him and he used them occasionally thereafter as a percussive device.

A situation his father had to cope with at one time in the Danbury Band amused and intrigued Charles Ives, and proved fertile for later musical treatment on a larger scale.

In a band whose members had attained only modest technical skill, individual temperament was bound to play a large part in performance. So it was not surprising that a nervous viola player, too shaky to look away from his score to follow the conductor, should tend to move at his own pace, winding up as a general thing several measures ahead of everybody else. Around the same time the band leader was plagued with a lethargic character who played the horn. He was equally unable to divide his attention between music stand and conductor, so he took what was for him a comfortable pace whenever the music got a little difficult, and he stuck to it, through thick and thin, so consistently that in several pieces it became the regular procedure for the band to play its cadence with a flourish and then wait quietly at attention (arms akimbo was customary) until the horn player got through *his* last two measures alone.

This of course provoked smiles, but it seemed to Charles Ives desirable that people should not all be alike; he found it reasonable therefore for a composer to allow for individual variation in performance, with respect both to tempo and to dynamics. The apparently insoluble problem of performing such music with a single conductor can be met easily if the orchestra is divided as Ives intended, under two leaders. The two parts of the orchestra then go their separate ways, coinciding perhaps at certain points, perhaps not. This is extremely difficult to write down and to read, but if the music is understood as having been intended to move along freely, each group taking its own tempo for a certain space, so that the important thing is the horizontal line and its forward-moving drive, the perpendicular collisions are immaterial, and the music is not at all difficult to manage in performance.

One of the types of polyphony that Ives uses had its prototype at a dance where by mistake two rival fiddlers had been invited to preside. Each stood his ground and played his particular version of the tune announced, with his special variations; the tunes were recognizably the same and yet the two fiddlers hardly ever played the same note at the same time. It seemed chaos to the ear, but it actually was not, since the two strands could be shown to be related.

Ives's use of quotation has been much commented upon and little understood. Emerson devoted an entire essay to *Quotation and Originality,* in which he said 'borrowing can come of magnanimity and stoutness . . .' He believed it important to the growth and continuity of man's thought: 'You do not quote, but recognize your own.' Quotation has been a literary device for generations: at least one book of Chaucer's is as complete a tissue of allusion as the works of Joyce and T. S. Eliot in the twentieth century. But music has frowned on it, and quotation from other composers has as a rule been unconscious. Ives, however, uses musical reminiscence as a kind of stream-of-consciousness device that brings up old tunes with their burden of nostalgic emotion. These snatches of hymns, minstrel songs, college songs, fiddle tunes, and so on, sewn through the fabric of his music, are never left as quotations only; certain fragments soon develop a life of their own, and some aspect of their musical structure is always made the basis of the piece's subsequent behavior, so that ultimately the music stands independent of any literary or other extra-musical connection.

Occasionally he makes his feeling more precise, as, for instance, when he adds the words of a stanza of *Watchman, tell us of the night,* to the score in the Fourth Violin Sonata, with no idea that they should be sung, but only to suggest what is going through the composer's mind at that point.

On a slightly different level, the presentation of the words recalls his father's practice of playing a fine hymn tune on the French horn, before a congregation each of whom was repeating the familiar words silently to himself; this is still deeply moving to Ives in retrospect. It gave him the idea for what he calls 'songs without voices.'

Of his appropriation of Beethoven's motif for the Fifth Symphony he has said that when, in the search for absolute law, the individual feels blocked, insufficient, and bound, he then may turn for liberation to greater souls, rather than to the external. Not that any true composer takes his substance from another, only that the ideas of a man of greater stature may prove a point of departure. So Ives had no compunction about using the motif of the Fifth Symphony as the motif on which he built the *Concord Sonata* (although actually it never once appears in exactly the form used by Beethoven). Ives did this out of no spirit of imitation or competition, but because he feels so great a theme is universal in nature, and that its implications should continue to grow and to be incorporated into new music.

All these aspects of his highly individual approach to music can be seen as clear and consistent when one remembers that to the Transcendentalist, music is not separate from the rest of the universe but permeates and is in turn permeated by all else that exists. For Ives, music is no more an expression of the universe than the universe is an expression of music.

Ives is not much interested in defining *American* music; there is nothing of the chauvinist about him. He has seemed to feel that any composer, no matter where he is born, who is preoccupied with the forms and the expression of human freedom and independence, who is capable of an exalted religious emotion, and who is fearless before the new and untried, cannot help writing *American* music because 'those are the qualities that have made America great.' He once wrote, in this connection:

> If the Yankee can reflect the fervency with which his gospels were sung — the fervency of Aunt Sarah, who scrubbed her life away for her brother's ten orphans, the fervency with which this woman, after a 14-hour work day on the farm, would hitch up and drive 5 miles through the mud and rain to prayer-meeting — her one articulate outlet for the fullness of her unselfish soul — if he can reflect the fervency of such a spirit, he may find there a local color that will do all the world good. If his music can but catch that spirit by being a part with itself, it will come somewhere near this idea — and it will be American, too. In other words, if local color, national color, any color, is a true pigment of the universal color, it is a divine quality. And it is a part of substance in art, not of manner.

Polyphony

Ives has never deliberately turned his style backward toward eras long past. His music reflects his own nineteenth-century musical background. It is not surprising, therefore, that in spite of the great variety of musical means that he uses, he never developed any feeling for the ecclesiastical modes and has not used them. Nor did he ever use modal counterpoint. In fact one gathers that organized counterpoint was not meaningful to him in spite of his studies; he never seems to have acquired a feeling for melodic association according to rule.

On the other hand, he often shows a great feeling for the independence of certain melodic lines and blocks of chords set against each other in polyphonic movement. (Sometimes these lines are bound together by huge harmonic or polyharmonic complexes.) The more familiar the melodic lines are, the more reasonable it seems to Ives to put them together with a special independence: each with its own key and perhaps also its own rhythm. In *In the Inn* there is such a spot near the end, in which the tune of the fast barn dance continues merrily against snatches from *We Won't Go Home until Morning* and *Good-night, Ladies.* Similarly, the final measures of the Second Symphony introduce the army reveille call against *Columbia, the Gem of the Ocean,* which has previously acted as *cantus firmus* for fragments of Bach and Brahms melodies.

Probably Ives's most characteristic and unusual independent use of melodies against each other comes from repeating, either exactly or sequentially — and often with rhythmic variation — the same few tones. When this is done in several parts independently, the result is a typically Ivesian web of melodic and rhythmic polyphony, since it is usually arranged so that the phases of the various re-

Ex. 1. From *Emerson.*

peating fragments never come out twice alike. Example 1 is a small portion of such a section, beginning in simple rhythm, then adding a syncopation on off-beat eighths. An extension of this idea appears in Ex. 2 (pp. 153–4), where there are twenty rhythmically independent voices, some single, some in block chords. The trombones are playing a tune based on *Marching through Georgia;* each of the other parts is playing its own short melodic phrase over and over, combining in different simultaneous keys and rhythms to form a complex polyphonic background.

It will be seen that in both these examples a ground-bass form is used, as in a passacaglia. Canonic imitation is not very frequent with Ives. His voices often answer each other with different forms of the same tune, in fuguing-tune fashion; they seldom repeat exactly the same way. On the rare occasions when he attempts conventional contrapuntal writing, there is a strong feeling of imprisonment in a form not naturally and simply felt by the composer.

The third movement of the Fourth Symphony is a fugue on a chordal hymn tune (Ex. 3, p. 154) with four entrances: tonic, dominant, tonic, dominant. The disposition of the counter-subject is unconventional, but not very much so; and although keys get buffeted about a bit in the free development, the whole thing does not depart very greatly from familiar fugal practice. Somehow the music seems far too cramped, as though he did not really wish to stay within the confines of a fugue but was for some reason forced to keep his wings tied. One misses the freedom of fancy. The tiny stretto in the last few measures of the fugue seems especially bound down.

Ives did his best work in creating constant new forms of his own as his musical concept demanded; it is generally true that the forms of canon, fugue, and all forms of strict imitation prove unsatisfactory in his hands. His free use of grounds, on the other hand, in different simultaneous rhythmic phases, are in his works a never-ending source of vitality and polyphonic unity.

Ex. 2. From Fourth Symphony.

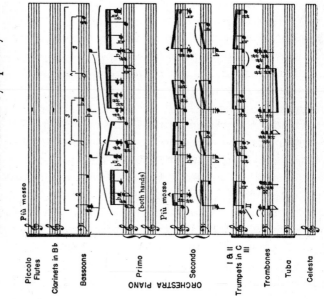

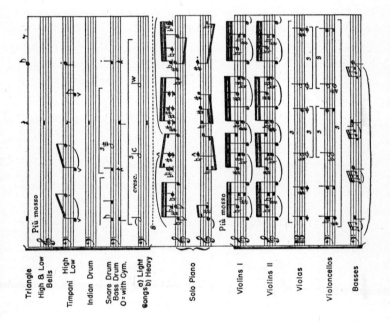

Ex. 3. From Fourth Symphony, 3rd Movement.

Some critics have had the impression that the various simultaneous voices and blocks of tones are entirely unrelated. Careful listening and examination of the scores do not bear this out, however. There are always relationships to be found; they are usually built on a rather complex harmonic concept.

The beginning of the song *Paracelsus* is a good example. As mentioned in its analysis later, the second measure of this song is written in a sort of polycounterpoint. There are three independent sets of chord blocks. If one were to select an essential tone from each chord, there would be three-part dissonant counterpoint (Ex. 4). Ives's sense of dissonant counterpoint is in fairly close accord with its formulation in the present-day teaching of modern ma-

Ex. 4. From *Paracelsus*.

terials. His feeling for it, used independently by him at about the time it was being developed in California and Germany by other people, is much stronger than for the classical counterpoint of his formal studies.

One of the typical Ives styles that is partly polyphonic, partly harmonic, is that in which he weaves a fabric with many different note-values at the same time, each part sustaining its own line. While the voices are quite separate, they are often also figurations of chord fragments, and the total, while polyphonic in general, forms an involved harmonic web and is in itself a sort of super-figuration. Each one of the many simultaneous parts is usually found to be a series of chordal leaps rather than any other sort of melodic progression. This is true of the sound-fabric woven in *The Housatonic at Stockbridge,* one of the *Three Places in New England,* and of a similar one in *In the Night.* Often in such a sound-web there is a main melody (sometimes a quotation), and the rest of the web is in the nature of an accompaniment. So it is evident that even when Ives's voices seem most independent, the melodies are bound together by a strong harmonic feeling, rather than being deliberately separated so as to be heard contrapuntally.

Harmony

At a time when consecutive extreme dissonances were unknown, Ives used them constantly whenever, in his judgment, they constituted the most powerful harmonic force for his purpose. He had no sense of their being ugly, or undesirable, or in any way unpleasant. In the same way, at a time when consecutive straight consonance was very little used (most other composers having temporarily decided in favor of constant mild sevenths and ninths), Ives used consonance whenever it seemed to him to belong to his musical intention.

Ives has always had a strong interest in harmony, and he has used all sorts and conditions of chords, making new ones of his own freely if he was tired of the old ones, but using the old ones, too, whenever they especially appealed to him. Not only has he used greater extremes of dissonance and consonance than were to be found elsewhere at the time, but he has also used more different chords — and more different sorts of chords — than can be found in the work of any other one composer one can think of.

One reason for this is that he was not restrained by any need for resolving dissonances. Except where he wished to recall older practice, the dissonant tones do not resolve downward stepwise, nor is there any feeling of expectation that they should. This failure to resolve active tones does not give any sense that his tonal obligations remain unfulfilled, however. Ives achieves, instead, an independence of dissonance in several different ways. There may be atonality (no one key center), but this is comparatively rare; he is more likely to retain the feeling of the key by keeping constantly before the ear the relation of each chromatic tone to its tonal center. He is apt so to arrange chord complexes that even if most of the chromatic tones are present — and no specific resolution of any of them is offered or expected — there yet remains a strong impression of a tonal center in the background. Often, of course, the picture is complicated by the existence of more than one key center at a time, when the melody lines or chord block lines are multiplied.

The three *Harvest Home Chorales,* for brass choir, string bass, organ, and mixed chorus show this block harmonic treatment. Strange sustained dissonances create a bed of sound on which the serious choral lines lie, with their contrasting very large and very small intervals, from semitones to leaps of a seventh. The accompanying instrumental lines are diatonic, but do not suggest keys. Toward the climax of the first Chorale, the singers chant without specified rhythm on the same dissonance with which the brasses opened, and the trumpets and trombones are set in counterpoint against each other in a series of perfect fifths which sound a magnificent fortissimo, making a triumphant climax against the monotony of the choir. In the second Chorale there are slow-moving major triads which melt into minor chords on the same root. The tenor enters with a melody in a slow rhythm of three, and a pizzicato bass plays nine equal notes set evenly across two measures. There is an inexorable flowing movement hastening on the pace to a tempo which is rapid without losing its ceremonial dignity in praise of the Lord of the Harvest. The final Chorale returns to an andante movement: the brass weaves a web of dissonant counterpoint, after which the voices enter a measure apart with a short fuguing tune, so that the effect is almost like a stretto. This is also somewhat dissonant, but it affords a contrast with the free dissonant counterpoint of the brass; with long sustained concords in the organ, it leads to the last chord, which contains simultaneously the tonic, dominant, and subdominant chords of the key of C major — a symbol of universal praise.

Although Ives does sometimes seem to arrive at a given harmonic treatment through some kind of improvisatory intuition, he seems more often to build his elaborate harmonic architecture through various kinds of structural analogy. For example, the song *Soliloquy* (Ex. 5) one page long, is described by Ives as 'an attempt at a take-off of the Yankee drawl . . . a study in sevenths and other things.' It is an extremely condensed exploration of the possibilities of building chords on intervals and in ways that produce startling new chord types, without ever deviating more than a little at any one point from the usual. The extraordinary thing is that one can find in this one-page song harmonic usages that characterize the music of many a later musical explorer who achieved fame before Ives.

Soliloquy begins with a major triad built with a major plus a minor third in the ordinary way. The next chord is a

Ex. 5. Soliloquy, or a Study in 7ths and Other Things.

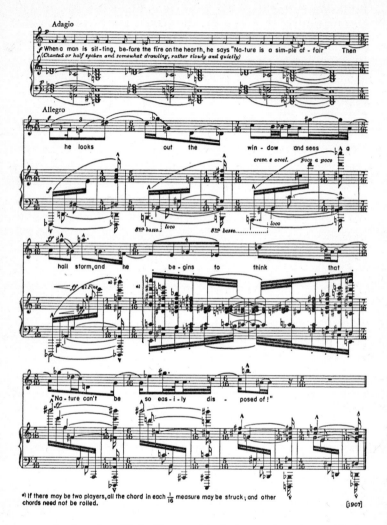

*) If there may be two players, all the chord in each $\frac{1}{16}$ measure may be struck; and other chords need not be rolled.

[1907]

seventh chord, still built on thirds but using both diminished and augmented thirds in addition to the first two

kinds. Next comes a thirteenth chord built in major and minor; this is enlarged into a seventeenth chord by doubling the first and third tones in a higher range, altered chromatically; they are sounded simultaneously with the unaltered first and third tones of the chord that are sounded in the lower register.

Following this there is a section devoted to various mixed chords built on major sevenths, minor ninths, and triads, after which comes a measure with successive chords built on minor sevenths, perfect fifths, perfect fourths, alternate major and minor thirds, major seconds, minor seconds, in that order. Then the series is reversed, building from minor seconds up to sevenths again. This is followed by a chord built downward (instead of upward as is customary) in major sevenths, a similar one in minor ninths, one built (downward still) with alternate perfect and augmented fourths (a type Schoenberg developed later) and continuing in sevenths. And finally there is a chord built in fourths, thirds, and sevenths, mixing all three of the basic interval systems together. Most of these chords had already appeared here and there in Ives's music, and he was to continue to use them; this song is a single example of their systematic organization.

Elsewhere in Ives's music the more complex chords are usually mixed-interval inventions of his own or else they are polychords, in which two or more simple chords are so placed against each other that they remain independent units instead of forming a single complex (Ex. 6). Aside from such mixtures, one finds occasionally huge chord-complexes built on a single interval, usually seconds (major or minor, or both) that form tone-clusters (Ex. 7). Sometimes thirds are mixed and massed in the same way (Ex. 8).

Ives customarily changes the number of voices in successive chords drastically. He has no feeling for the idea that

159

one should have continuous four or any other consistent number of parts, in the harmony. Example 9 shows an eight-part, a fifteen-part, and a five-part chord, one after the other.

Ex. 6. From *Paracelsus*.

Ex. 7. From *The Majority*.

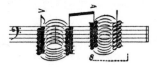

Ex. 8. From *The Majority*.

Ex. 9. From *Paracelsus*.

As to the ways in which he makes his chord connections, Ives is consistent about using whichever connections he feels best fit his musical intention. Nothing is excluded as unfit for consideration. In his studies, Ives learned to write very well according to the rules of conventional harmony and counterpoint. In fact, he frequently mentions as proof of the intelligence of his father's teaching that he was required to show skill in handling musical materials conventionally before writing in any other way. In his creative work, Ives developed a rule of his own, however. The rule is that he will follow consistently whatever type of harmonic organization he has decided at the beginning will be most appropriate to his musical idea.

For example, in the song *Walt Whitman* he followed his rule by using parallel fifths and octaves; any other kind of chord would have violated it (Ex. 10). In the song *Memories,* on the other hand, the rules of the free creation and the rules of the school books happen to coincide; he avoids parallel fifths and octaves here (Ex. 11). In both cases, only the simplest chords were required. In *Walt Whitman,* chords without thirds seemed more fitting; in *Memories,* the chords contain their thirds.

Ex. 10. From *Walt Whitman.*

Ex. 11. From *Memories.*

Ives, intensely religious himself, has expressed vigorous opinions about the habit of harmonizing hymns with a few well-worn and 'easy' chords, thus narrowing down an expression that should be expanding and universal in scope. His early rather primitive experiments, when he simply added another third to the triads used for *Nearer, My God, to Thee,* were followed by more carefully composed works, of which the *67th Psalm* is a fine example. Here the chorus is divided into two independent groups, each singing simple triads in three parts. The two groups never sing the same triad at the same time, however, so there is a constant polyharmony between the parts. This does not usually mean that two different keys are involved, but rather that different simultaneous simple chords flow past each other in the same key. The effect is one of mysterious grandeur: God's universe seems wider and less personal than it does when a congregation sings its homey, old-fashioned hymns.

Example 12 shows an assortment of unusual single chord

Ex. 12. From *Paracelsus.*

connections chosen from different works, illustrating the variety of treatment to be found in Ives's music and ranging from the familiar simple varieties to the more characteristic large chord-complexes.

Melody

Ives's own melodies are less unusual than what he does with them. He likes to develop a melody sonata fashion — that is, he takes a short motif as a germ (Ex. 13), extends it into a theme, and the theme into a longer melody, little by little. Usually the germ of the melodic idea is quite simple, but sometimes a comparatively complicated version of it is presented before the simplest form is disclosed, since Ives habitually regards clarity as an ultimate, not a beginning.

Ex. 13. From *Paracelsus.*

In the extension of his motifs, Ives sometimes employs melodic inversion, retrograde and inverted retrograde — the primary permutations that were often used by sixteenth-century composers but had been lost sight of in the nineteenth century and only reappeared in Europe when they were applied to twelve-tone rows by Schoenberg. Ives uses them for the extension of shorter motifs, and he also draws freely on the rarer secondary permutations (where part of the motif may remain, part be inverted). *Paracelsus* offers examples of this.

He is also fond of rhythmic augmentation and diminution of short motifs. With inversion and retrograde, these various related shapes of the same melody are used by Ives to build up what he regards as a work's essential unity, not according to any artificial system, but because these ways of development serve to present many sides of the whole. This Ives considers indispensable to a true understanding of the meaning of the music, just as he believes no truth in any other field can be arrived at without the examination of many points of view about it. Anything that presents many facets of an idea, musical or otherwise, is always eagerly seized on and built into his thinking immediately.

Ives has also, though rarely, extended his melody lines by taking tones whose first appearance is in ordinary scale-wise passages and shifting their octave level upon repetition of the passage. This too is often to be found in Schoenberg, rarely before him (Ex. 21, p. 193).

The beginning point of an Ives melody is more apt to be a quotation than not, and Ives utilizes to the full the nostalgic quality thus incorporated into his music, playing upon the listener's feelings through association. The quoted tunes, though often obvious in origin, are never disclosed in just the same form as the original. Fragments of a certain tune may appear a hundred times in the course of a single movement, but never twice exactly the same. Either the rhythm will be changed, or the tune will go off into a new key in the middle or will continue into a fragment from something else. Ives finds a thousand different ways of continuing the music. There are threads of old hymns running through nearly every serious movement, to such an extent that one is tempted to see in this music a Protestant parallel to the permeation of secular music in Europe by the Gregorian chant.

Ives's melodies often change key implication very rapidly, so that in spots they may suggest atonality. Usually, however, they are plainly major, minor or chromatic; rarely are they modal or genuinely atonal.

Since Ives has no feeling against training his concordant old sacred tunes to spread along dissonant chord lines, it may frequently happen that some old motifs (in themselves perfectly circumspect, falling along simple scale or chord lines) may grow into modern-sounding music with greatly widened outlines. His nineteenth-century motif then becomes a twentieth-century melody with a wide span and dissonant polyphonic or polytonal implications. When this practice is based on an underlying familiar tune, association illuminates the music and gives a basis for emotional understanding, even if the structure embraces new concepts as well as old ones. Nowadays, when the particular tunes Ives knew are less familiar than they were, the idiom still carries its burden of feeling for all of us.

Rhythm

Ives's occasional complexity of rhythm has become a byword. It is true that it is in some spots and in some ways probably more involved than that to be found in any other written music. Thinking to find an illustration, I opened the score of the last movement of the Fourth Symphony at random, and I immediately came upon a measure, the first on page 24, which, nominally in 3/2 meter, proves to have twenty different simultaneous rhythmic figures, with three, four, five, and six notes of equal value filling the measure in different voices, the rest of the figures being made up of notes of unequal value.

At sight of the second movement of the Fourth Symphony, every orchestra conductor exclaims at once: 'Impossible to conduct the piece!' When early in 1927 the score was shown to Eugene Goossens, he said exactly the same thing, but thereafter he proceeded differently from other people, for he wound a towel about his head, drank gallons of coffee, sat up nights, learned the score, and found a way to conduct it successfully in public.

It is hard to blame conductors for their reaction. This second movement is set at M.M. ♩. (of 6/8) = about 50. Its pages open with equal eighth notes, 6/8 meter in the solo piano, percussion, brass, flutes and piccolo. A 5/8 meter is assigned to clarinet, second orchestra piano, triangle and bells; 7/4 to the bassoons; and 2/4 to the first orchestra piano. Against this, the upper strings have a measure equal to twelve of the eighth notes previously mentioned, but written as a whole note to a measure; and the bass viols have a free part with no bar lines, but with the eighth note duration the same, note for note, as in the solo piano part.

In case this rhythmic scheme has begun to seem dull, there is encouragement in the solo piano part, where one hand plays 3/4 against the other hand's 6/8, and there are various gruppetti: 4 notes in the time of 3 (solo piano part, second measure), 2 equal notes in the time of 5/8 (second orchestra piano, third measure). And so on and so on.

When Nicolas Slonimsky conducted *Washington's Birthday* he gave seven beats with the baton (in itself not a thing every conductor finds simple), three with his left hand, and led two beats by nodding his head. This created both great amusement and great admiration and is a tale still often told.

The unusual and occasionally unique features of Ives's rhythm may be divided into several categories.

The first is concerned with meter, particularly irregular meter. Such signatures as 5/8, 7/8, 10/8, 11/8, 9/8, with irregular groupings of notes within the measures, also 5/4, 7/4, 5/2, 7/2, 9/2, and meters with fractional beats such as 6½/2 (p. 9, last movement, Fourth Symphony) are not uncommon, and are to be found in Ives's music beginning in the early 1890's.

He applies to these meters types of development that may be described as melodic (variety of successive meters in a single line), harmonic (variety of simultaneous meters related perpendicularly), and contrapuntal (in which several horizontal lines with changing meters are set against each other, with relationships that appear consecutively in the various voices instead of simultaneously).

The changes in metric signature have to do with schematic accentuation, of course. He does not usually use such a metrical signature as 6/4 to indicate triplet quarter notes (as Wagner sometimes did). Rather Ives is addicted to the general twentieth-century practice of using a constant unit (usually an eighth note) to underlie all the different meters.

Once in a long while Ives slips back rather inconsistently to the Wagner concept, as in the violin parts on the first page of the score of the second movement of the Fourth Symphony. In such cases deciphering the rhythm is difficult indeed.

Another category of rhythm, dealing also with unusual accentuation, and of especial fascination to Ives, is one that includes off-beat accents and syncopation. Ives heard a great deal of minstrel music in his youth and was always alive to its off-beat rhythmic thrusts. In such of his movements as *In the Inn* and part of the First Piano Sonata, the Charleston rhythm (8/16 divided 3 plus 5) and the rumba rhythm (8/16 divided 3 plus 3 plus 2) may be found, long before these dances were generally known in the United States. Ives's fertility in inventing an almost unending number of similar sorts of rhythms is astonishing. His humorous movements, which occur in almost all the larger works, are full of such irregular off-beat stresses.

With respect to the duration of tones Ives has been highly creative too. Our present musical notation makes it easy to represent note-lengths that divide or multiply by 2 and by 3; these are all much used. They are fairly easy to write down when the figure starts on the beginning of a beat, or if the whole figure is completed on an off-beat. Gruppetti of fives, sevens, and higher uneven numbers become increasingly hard to use, of course. Ives, however, deals with all of them up to nine with great frequency, and with still higher numbers at times.

This does not mean only that he may have five notes on a beat. The five may be so divided that one note will con-

tain two of the five and a second note, three of the five.
That is, with the signature 2/2 one may have

$$\underset{5}{\overset{}{\text{♩. ♩}}}\,\underset{5}{\overset{}{\text{♩ ♩.}}}.$$

Such gruppetti do usually start on the beat, but there are many instances in which they are initiated off of the beat so that they begin and end somewhere between beats (Ex. 13). Some of his groups deal with extended lengths seldom seen elsewhere, such as a triplet two measures in length in 4/4 meter. Besides the more familiar triplets, Ives frequently writes 2, 4, or 8 even notes across a 3/8 or 3/4 measure.

In the employment of these many related different note lengths, Ives uses the same three general ways of development noted in the case of his meter: he sometimes changes succssively from one gruppetto to another, forming a horizontal or what I have called a 'melodic' relation between differing lengths; he sometimes uses several gruppetti together simultaneously, so that the note-lengths have a harmonic relationship (that is to say the different lengths are so related perpendicularly that the whole sounds unified); and sometimes he does both of these things at once, forming a polyrhythmic association not unlike that of counterpoint in tonal relationships.

In the three parts of the *Theatre or Chamber Orchestra Set* one may discover several different kinds of rhythmic treatment. This *Set* was written in 1906, when it was not at all customary for symphonists to write for small orchestra; but Ives used often to pinch-hit as conductorpianist in a theater orchestra led by a friend; he grew accustomed to the size of the group and liked the variety of instrumentation possible with it.

The first movement, *In the Cage,* was suggested by a walk Ives took with Bart Yung (one of the Poverty Flat friends, who was half Chinese) in Central Park. They sat for a while in the Zoo, watching a small boy who was in turn watching the endless pacing to and fro of a caged leopard; and it occurred to Yung to wonder whether all three observers were not equally caged without knowing it. The music reproduces the regular padding of the leopard's paws in triplets, but against this there are nervous chords and a counterpoint that change meter with every measure. In the introduction there is one of Ives's famous 'firsts': a series of notes that become successively shorter, a half, a dotted quarter, a quarter, a dotted eighth, an eighth, and a sixteenth. (This is the sort of time-value succession advocated by the French *Musique Concrète* group in 1952.)

In the Inn, the second movement, was suggested by the sounds that come from inside the inn to the ear of a passer-by. But certainly in 1906 no ragtime was ever quite so syncopated. Nearly every note is wildly off-beat. The opening measures divide a group of 8 sixteenth notes into 3 plus 3 plus 2 — in other words, this is the rumba rhythm introduced in the United States by Afro-Cubans more than thirty years later. The last four measures are called a chorus, and Ives gives four optional ways of playing the third measure from the end; the performer may share in the creative process by selecting the one he prefers. (Part of this movement turns up in the First Piano Sonata.)

The last part, *In the Night,* is one of Ives's mysterious tonal webs, woven of six or seven very soft, slow-moving, independent parts. No one tonality emerges: the leading voices play an ostinato figure, each in its own key. The horn has a solo melody against all this, and words are indicated — a 'song without voice' for the horn player to think as he plays, about getting scared in the dark.

The First Piano Sonata and *Tone Roads No. 3* each

illustrate ways of organizing rhythmic ideas through a whole work that are parallel to, without being identical with, those in the *Theatre Orchestra Set*. The Sonata begins majestically, adagio con moto, immediately complex in its use of rapidly shifting dissonance in never-ending lines, with no sense of any tonal center. The rhythm is not so involved as in other works, but this movement has the peculiar combination of excitement and the grand manner that is also to be found in the first movement of the Second Piano Sonata (the *Concord*).

The second movement, allegro moderato, is a tiny, animated, syncopated scherzo in the form of a verse and chorus. The verse is a travesty on *How Dry I Am;* the chorus uses a highly ornamented version of *O Susanna* as a base — although one is hardly aware of this through the complexities of the accompanying figures. The largo which follows is, like the first movement, a grand, flowing, dissonant movement, based largely on the gong-like resonance of superimposed fifths, with shifting moods and melodies.

The fourth movement, allegro, goes from one extreme form of syncopation to another; its super-jazziness is descended from minstrel-show music, carried to an unheard-of point. The rhythms of five and three against four, and so on, are not in a hazy tangle as in Ives's slow, moody music (e.g. *In the Night* in the *Theatre Orchestra Set*), but are crackling and clear, punctuated by sharp accents, usually on off-beats. Rows of small secundal chords are used to add to the general belligerence. The last movement, andante maestoso, starts rather like the first and third movements, with rhapsodic phrases and changes of speed. It grows into a tricky syncopated allegro dance, to make a bright and showy climax to the sonata. Its opening is tonally complex, the ending simpler. Dissonances are not fundamental but are used to worry and harass the tonality, 'pulling the ears around' as Ives likes to do. The rhythm is full of darting, live, irregular thrusts.

When Ives calls a piece 'tone roads,' he means something for a combination of instruments in which the tone color of one of them gives its character to the sound all the way through. Some of his finest music is to be found among such pieces for miscellaneous chamber combinations (which sometimes include the voice). These works are seldom heard because it is so expensive to gather just the right group of players for such short things, when there is no other music for the same combination to fill out a program.

Tone Roads No. 3 (for flute, clarinet, trumpet, trombone, chimes, piano, and strings) opens with a long solo in slow half-note and whole-note triplets, an atonal melody played by the chimes, which provide the tone quality that is to lie back of the whole piece. The 'tone road' is the tone of the chime, and the whole is a fantasy on the mood of the chime tone. Chime tones are in themselves a rather dissonant complex, but they can hardly have been used in atonal melody with wide dissonant leaps before.

When the trombone joins the chimes, it does so in a counter-melody of stuttering rhythmical figures based on a rhythm of five against the chimes' three, and when the trumpet joins in, its melody has a rhythm of four against the other two. The clarinet soon adds a counterpoint of rapid syncopation. When the piano comes in with a series of low major seventh chords that suggest the tone of the chimes, the rhythm changes to 3/4, with the piano playing dotted eighth notes, and the trombone hurrying his groups of five so that they fit into a 3/4 measure instead of the earlier 4/4. When the flute brings in its independent melody in fast triplets, there are six very individual strands of melody in dissonant counterpoint, dominated by the all-penetrating chimes as a binding force. The trio increases in speed and with the help of the strings builds up to nine-part counterpoint. Then the chimes stop for a moment, the other parts go wildly every which way, until at the end the chimes reappear as a catalyst to crystallize the sound of the other instruments into sense.

Examples of all these usages may be found in the two published movements of the Fourth Symphony and in *The Housatonic at Stockbridge*. In his *Universe Symphony* Ives has indicated some slight use of both the metric and tone-duration counterpoint simultaneously. This is, of course, extremely involved, and examples are rare. Ives has never carried out this idea consistently.

At the other end of the range of possibilities, there are cases where there is no particular metrical organization, regular or irregular. Here Ives leaves out the metrical signature, and he has either no bar lines at all or else he sets them irregularly where he wishes the impression of a first beat. This is a prose concept of rhythm; it is also related to the idea that different stresses may be given by different performers, all of them right. The *Emerson* movement of the *Concord Sonata* affords an example.

In some cases one may feel a constant uninterrupted succession of strong beats (as in the *Emerson* movement, page 3, system 3). But usually one feels that Ives hopes to induce the performer not to be too bound by any one way of organizing strong and weak beats, playing the passages now one way, now another.

Ives's whole approach to his complex rhythms should be understood as an attempt to persuade players away from the strait-jacket of regular beats, with which complete exactness is impossible anyhow, and to induce them to play with rubato in the involved places, with a freedom that creates the impression of a sidewalk crowded with individuals who move forward with a variety of rhythmic tensions and muscular stresses that make constant slight changes of pace. In fact, Ives has often expressed regret at having to write out a piece at all, since its rhythms will then be hopelessly crystallized.

In spite of his concept of freedom for the performer in those spots where equal collaboration between composer and performer seems to him desirable, Ives has no patience at all with changes to make playing easier. He has accepted the challenge of his involved notation for himself by showing that he can play the rhythms as he has written them, with surprising and meticulous accuracy. In the orchestra works, of course, where there are sometimes twenty or more simultaneous rhythms going on, absolute accuracy would be not only impossible to achieve in performance, but in Ives's view unnecessary, since the complexity arises from a concept of individual freedom. He is well satisfied, on the whole, if the sense and feeling of the idea can be seen and heard in the mind by a fellow score-reader. Physical realization in performance is far less important to him.

Form

As indicated earlier, Ives's aim is not to make the form simple and clear, but rather to create an underlying unity out of a large number of diverse elements, used assymmetrically; he thus relates his music by analogy to the individual's experience of life. The sense of unity is not brought about through exact repetition, either of motifs or of sections, but is established through relationships. And Ives prefers that these relationships should not be too obvious.

There must always be something for the mind and feeling to work on, some new aspect of relationship to be found. If everything is self-evident, that spiritual inactivity that Ives so abhors might be induced.

So in such works as the *Concord Sonata* or the Fourth Symphony there is nearly always a great deal going on. There will be many sections of contrasting lengths. There will be a first theme and a contrasting second theme, and perhaps still further themes, although in the development of a single theme there may be so many aspects disclosed which suggest the theme to follow that one is hardly aware of the moment when the new theme is exposed. One side of the form may be related to chords (hardly ever the tonic and dominant, however). One aspect nearly always concerns the development and expansion of a melodic motif or motifs, while another concerns rhythmical figures and *their* development and expansion.

Ives has a sense akin to Beethoven's of the recapitulation of the main motif as the moment of the most intense drama; but the position of this return is not likely to be in the conventionally assigned spot. In the first movement of the *Concord Sonata,* for instance, this dramatic point comes on the page just before the end, instead of being made into a full section. And instead of having the second theme developed after the first, in the return, both are developed together. This results in a far greater dramatic concentration of forces than is usual.

Some of Ives's works written in the 'nineties make a good starting point in studying his form, since they may be for the most part quite simple and symmetrical and yet contain some single characteristic off-balance element.

In the song *Karen* there is a four measure introduction, with the first two measures repeated exactly. The voice part is in four phrases, the first three of which are four measures long; the third phrase is built on the same melody as the first, but with some rhythmical change and a different cadence. The fourth phrase is not actually very different in length from the others, but after three phrases in 3/4 the fourth phrase changes to four measures of 3/8 followed by one of 4/4. On the last note of the phrase, the 3/4 resumes again, the piano recapitulating its introductory phrase for four measures. The very last measure, by way of surprise, echoes the first measure softly an octave higher. Since the chord scheme has been two beats of tonic followed by one beat of dominant this brings the little song to a close on the dominant seventh chord.

Many of the other songs in the collection *114 Songs* can be analyzed somewhat similarly: there will be, in the early ones, a conventional form as basis, but there will also always be some slight deviation. The German settings capture the spirit of German lieder very well, but in *Weil' auf Mir* all the phrases are four measures long, as is suggested by the regular meter of the poem, except the second phrase, in both stanzas, which is only three measures long, although there is nothing in the poem to suggest such a difference. Conventional as the rest of the music is, with an accompaniment in an unbroken flow of sixteenth notes, the irregularity of the three-measure phrase stands out strongly.

The works called sonatas and symphonies do not necessarily have two contrasting themes in the first movement, the second in the dominant of the first, nor do they necessarily have clear-cut A-B-A sections, or follow other parts of the school-book sonata form. Ives is not alone in this, of course; it would be difficult indeed to find any important piece of music written during the last 150 years that does follow that form precisely. However, Ives follows the general principle of sonata form in works bearing these titles, in the sense that he applies the principle of contrasting ideas that develop toward unity.

Such a development, in a typical Ives composition, is not confined to the first movement but operates through the work as a whole. In the *Concord Sonata,* for example, the main motif, that of Beethoven's Fifth Symphony, acts as an integrating factor throughout, bringing together the seemingly contrasting ideas in both music and philosophy. Ives has marked the contrasting sections in the first movement as 'verse' and 'prose,' and has written at length in his notes and essays on the differences in philosophy and personality between the Concord figures after whom the movements are named. In the Fourth Symphony, various contrasts are presented in the first three movements, and are all resolved together in the last movement. The first movement is chromatic, the third movement diatonic; the second movement is jerky, syncopated, and complex in rhythm, the third movement smooth and simple rhythmically. The second movement is secular, related to dance music, and the third movement is religious and song-like. All these characteristics are combined into a steady musical flow in the fourth movement, which is perfectly unified in sound despite the complexity of its make-up. Even the humor of the second movement and the gravity of the third reappear together. Ives would not be his paradoxical self if he did not show that church-going may have its lighter side and fun-making be profound.

One of Ives's most spectacular achievements is the invention of a form which logically uses consonance and dissonance in a single piece; this occurs in the music for small orchestra called *The Unanswered Question.* The orchestra is divided, the strings playing very softly throughout off-stage, representing the silence of the seers who, even if they have an answer, cannot reply; the wind group, on stage, is dominated by the trumpet, which asks the Perennial Question of Existence over and over in the same way, while 'the Fighting Answerers (flutes and other people)' run about trying in vain to discover the invisible, unattainable reply to the trumpet. When they finally surrender the search they mock the trumpet's reiteration and depart. The Question is then asked again, for the last time, and the 'silence' sounds from a distance undisturbed.

Silence is represented by soft slow-moving concordant tones widely spaced in the strings; they move through the whole piece with uninterrupted placidity. After they have gone on long enough to establish their mood, loud wind instruments cut through the texture with a dissonant raucous melody that ends with the upturned inflection of the Question. At first the Question is asked briefly and infrequently, the quiet strings emerging in between; but the Question soon becomes more insistent, louder, longer, oftener heard; and it arouses more and more dissonance in the other wind instruments each time. When the dissonant voices disappear, the faint consonant chords continue to hum softly in the distance, like the eternal music of the spheres.

Instrumentation and Voice Writing

In examining Ives's writing for instruments and for the voice, it should be borne in mind that his early experience in playing and arranging for a great many different instruments equipped him thoroughly to know and to write entirely within the capacity of each instrument. Contemporary music in any era always presents greater technical difficulties than performers want or expect, but when Ives is writing music intended to be heard, the instruments or the voice have good individual parts and are placed where they sound well. There is nothing of the hit-or-miss in the scoring of the Second or Third Symphonies.

One of the reasons for the early and continued success of Ives's songs is their real feeling for the nature of the voice. As a rule, even if the voice part seems hard at first, it will sound fine when once it is well assimilated. Singers' chief difficulty is in finding the right tone against dissonant accompanying tones; it is primarily a task of musicianship that Ives has set.

On the other hand, Ives is violently contemptuous of passages written simply to sound well for the voice or the instrument. This is because he considers that the composer's job is to write *music*. This music is the *idea*. The idea should not be subordinated to techniques of performance, and it should never be changed for the sake of facility. In certain sorts of composition Ives makes a distinction between the music, which is the idea, and the sound, which is simply a physical disturbance during a performance. Naturally it is desirable to have the best sound possible, if this is compatible with the music. But the music itself must never be sacrificed. In *Essays Before a Sonata:*

> A manuscript score is brought to a concert master. He may be a violinist. He is kindly disposed. He looks it over and casually fastens on a passage: 'That's bad for the fiddle, it doesn't hang just right. Write it like this . . . they will play it better.' My God! What has sound to do with music! The waiter brings the only fresh egg he has, but the man at breakfast sends it back because it doesn't fit his egg cup. Why can't music go out the same way it comes in to a man, without having to crawl over a fence of sounds, thoraxes, catguts, wire,

wood and brass . . . The instrument! There is the perennial difficulty, there is music's limitations. Why must the scarecrow of the keyboard — the tyrant in terms of the mechanism (be it Caruso or a Jew's harp) — stare into every measure?

Some fiddler was once honest enough, or brave enough, or perhaps ignorant enough, to say that Beethoven didn't know how to write for the violin. That, maybe, is one of the reasons Beethoven is not a Vieux-temps. Another man says Beethoven's piano sonatas are not pianistic. With a little effort, perhaps, Beethoven could have become a Thalberg.

Some of Ives's Music of the Idea, therefore, was quite frankly written not so much to be sounded (though there is no objection to this if it proves possible) as to be perceived, to be heard in the mind's ear.

A piece with a great idea behind it that has proved possible to perform only by dint of immense determination in everyone concerned is *Lincoln, the Great Commoner,* a setting of the poem by Edwin Markham, for voices and orchestra. (It was also adapted for solo voice with piano, in the *114 Songs.*) It was planned for a group of voices, not only because a single voice would not be loud enough against a vivid, rhythmic, crashing orchestra, but also because the composer wished the vocal line to have the impersonal quality imparted by many voices. For the most part the singers are therefore in unison, but toward the end they break into shouted tone clusters, hard to sing at intervals of a second, but hair-raising when done as written, like the voice of a people, not the voice of a person.

At a point of climax on the word 'whirlwind' the first and second violins (each section divided into five parts that play in groups of consecutive seconds) dash about in contrary motion, with cross-rhythms based on fives and sevens, — the gruppetti of five often starting in the middle of the other group's seven. At the end the rhythm is unified, with great shouts in the voices and wide leaps to extended ranges, giving the feeling of superhuman energy, to which the orchestra adds huge accented dissonances by way of punctuation.

Lincoln is extraordinarily difficult, both for voices and instruments, but once accomplished it is one of the most unusual and exciting works in choral literature.

Ives himself has sometimes been willing to agree completely with conductors who have pointed out that certain passages in his music are too hard rhythmically to be performed exactly. He was, however, full of pleased astonishment when Eugene Goossens finally found a way to conduct an accurate performance of a nearly impossible spot. On the whole, however, he believes, as he has repeatedly written, that the impossibilities of today are the possibilities of tomorrow, and that the importance of the music's idea is bound to overcome the difficulties of the music's sound.

In these 'ideal' passages (but only there), one finds some parts in the fabric of the orchestra that do not balance and cannot be heard properly. The celesta is not normally audible above the trumpet, but Ives wishes the celesta tone-quality in the music, so he writes for an ideal celesta that *would* balance a loud trumpet, even though he knows perfectly well that it does not exist. Very often he needs flute-like tones balancing a brass section; when he wants this he writes for it. Bassoons, also, would often need to be louder than they are to balance properly, but he uses them anyway, with full knowledge of how they really sound. This kind of scoring is not found throughout his music, which would make it all impractical, but is reserved for certain sorts of especially 'idealistic' movements in which there is a transcendental summary and unification. The last movement of the Fourth Symphony and the *Universe Symphony* as it now stands, show such scoring. Whenever there is some good, practical way to gain his end, Ives of course does not resort to such unplayable writing. For example, in the song *The Majority* he believes that if the accompaniment is played as loudly as he wishes it to be, it will drown out any solo singer, so he recommends that the vocal line be taken by a unison chorus. So far as I know, no chorus has ever done so, but it is a perfectly practical idea.

The joke, of course, is really on those who would have composers write something suitable for their *instruments* when the *music* calls for something else. By sticking to his guns, Ives has lived into an age when singers are able to sing his songs, when players can play his rhythms (most of the time, at least), and when any desired orchestral balance is possible to achieve if one is willing to bother with electrical amplification to make audible any of the instrumental parts that do not now balance. The unheard tones of new and hitherto undreamed-of timbre that Ives imagines in his composer's mind, and that he wishes for his *Universe Symphony*, are certainly much closer to possible realization on electrical instruments — if these instruments were freed of the absurdity of imitating already known tone qualities — than in the old days of thorax and catgut.

X

Three Works Explored

'I CAN NEVER EXAGGERATE ENOUGH'

Paracelsus

This song (Ex. 14), written in 1921, is a setting of part of
Browning's poetic drama of that name. In its general form
the piece proceeds by degrees from loud to soft, from intense to calm, from complex to simple.

The main flow is in the piano part, which opens with six
and a half frenzied, tightly packed measures before the
voice begins. The thematic material separates itself fairly
obviously into several short motifs that are used in many
different forms. They all appear, actually, in the very first

Ex. 14. From *Paracelsus*.

* Taken from the latter part of Scene V   (Notes not marked otherwise are natural)

glo - ry vowed I soul and limb.___ Yet con-sti - tu-ted thus, and thus endowed, I failed:

I gazed ___ on power, I gazed ___ on

power till I grew ___ blind........... What wonder if I saw no way to shun despair? The

power I sought seemed God's..................... I learned my own deep er - ror; And

what pro - por - tion love should hold with power in man's right con - sti - tu - tion; Al - ways pre -

ce - ding power, And with much power,_____ al - ways, al - ways much more love;....

[1912-1921]

185

measure, some of them in more than one of their forms, most of them in their far from simplest aspect. The customary process, as so often with Ives, is reversed: the most complex weaving-about of the motifs comes right away in full force, with four-part polyphony that grows to five parts on the third beat and nine parts on the last beat. Enough material for an entire symphony is exposed in this measure alone. Instead of beginning with a simple motif and developing its implications, we start out here with several simultaneous complexities that have the air on first meeting of being in the final stages of their development. In the course of the song the threads are more and more simplified, and the more open, clear ideas emerge from behind the more involved ones.

In a large work one needs to have melodic motifs to work with that suggest the possibility of diatonic and chromatic conjunct motion, as well as perfect and imperfect concords in disjunct motion — this for the sake of completeness. Ives has evidently approached this three-page song in the same way. In the first measure the first two notes of the bass form a minor second; the next two continue and form another, but start a major second higher. Thus the whole step grows from the semitone, and together they form a compact four-note motif, the unity of which is emphasized by its immediate reappearance in sequence (in a different rhythm). The distance outlined between the outside tones of the motif form a diminished fourth (enharmonic major third) which begins to be developed harmonically in the tenor part in the second measure.

This opens up all classes of intervals except the perfect, which now, however, appears in the alto part; this part proceeds a perfect fourth up, followed at once by the melodic inversion beginning on the already established minor second above. These two contrasting motifs are the crux of the matter; the other motif forms are variations of them.

When the voice finally enters, it moves from B-flat to F, as in the alto's first melodic inversion; the F of the voice is followed by E, the melodic inversion of the opening bass motif, E to F. The voice then proceeds to develop the semitone, but changes the octave level from E-flat to D in the fashion made famous by Schoenberg. The major second is reversed for the end of the phrase.

Recurring motifs formed of various permutations of the conjunct intervals may be found before the voice enters. For example, the tenor opens with C, D-sharp, E. The first bass phrase ends with C, B, D-sharp, E — the inserted B making a variation. The soprano part opens with two semitones; in fact, semitones turn up several times in pairs. Perhaps the most frequently used secondary motif is that formed by the junction of the first bass motif and its sequence, which is a whole step (or its enharmonic equivalent) followed by the semitone between. Example 15 shows

Ex. 15. From *Paracelsus*.

some permutations of this motif encountered in the first three measures. Pairs of whole tones, some continuing in the same direction, others changing direction between the pairs, are also of frequent occurrence. Mixed whole and semitones in the same direction are often seen. Example 16 shows some of the forms that appear in the first measure, as well as later.

Ex. 16. From *Paracelsus*.

The second measure is still very complex, but the method of simplification begins to be disclosed. By the end of the first measure there are nine parts, but in the second measure these are formed into harmonic blocks. The three lower parts move together in a bass chord, the four higher parts move together in a soprano-alto chord, and there are two tenor parts that move together in thirds. The bass and tenor blocks are consonant; the soprano block is dissonant, a triad accompanied by the ninth in each case. The polychords formed by the simultaneous blocks are somewhat dissonant, but all may be considered related as ornamental tones of the progression of a dominant to a tonic to a dominant chord in the key of G. The various blocks move with so much independence that one may say they form a kind of polycounterpoint, in which each block is the equivalent of a single contrapuntal voice.

By the time the voice enters, the fabric has thinned down to four parts, with a few additional flurries of extra parts coming in and out. There are still a few blocks of sound, but we now have for the most part dissonant counterpoint in single lines. In the tenth measure, against the second vocal phrase, there is an enormous single block of thirds in the treble together with a large cluster of seconds in the bass, so that in spite of the continued large number of parts (15), a simplification has grouped them into two large and distinct chords against the vocal line and a single-voiced consonant counterpoint in the tenor. In the next measure eleventh chords are arranged so that they form a double row of consecutive fifths, against the voice and a high descant. By the end of the thirteenth measure there are still two simultaneous blocks of chords — this time one group built on fourths, the other on thirds plus a ninth — but they now move in similar motion together, in the course of the simplification, so that there is no longer any sense of contrapuntal relation between the blocks; instead there is the effect of dissonant harmony. By the fifteenth measure there are two blocks of plain triads placed against each other polyharmonically; no counterpoint. In the following measure, the polychords run together, forming simple chords in consonant accompaniment to the now simple tonal (key of G) vocal melody. Except for a few chromatic ornaments, this melody remains in key to the end, and while there is a slight reversion to mild chromatic chords in the piano just before the piece ends, the voice and the piano come together in a plain triad on D at the very close.

Ives characteristically does not use any metrical signature, but instead sprinkles bar lines about wherever he wishes to have an emphatic down beat. The first measure contains ten eighth notes, the second measure, fourteen; the third measure, eight; the next is twenty-five sixteenth notes in length. The shortest measure is three quarter notes long; the longest contains twenty-one quarter notes. These differences flow from the meaning and drama of the music rather than from any mathematical scheme; but the idea of asymmetrical sectional balances is very powerful here, as in many of Ives's form structures.

Rhythmical augmentation and diminution of motifs is frequent. In general, each melodic line or harmonic block moves with rhythmical independence, in polyphonic style, but in this song there is no particularly complex setting of unusual note values against each other. The very first quarter-note beat containing a quarter note in the soprano, a triplet (three twelfth notes) in the alto, two eighth notes in the tenor, and an eighth plus two sixteenths in the bass, is the moment of greatest rhythmic complication, in keeping with the over-all concept by which the most involved aspects begin the piece.

A characteristic example of Ives's way of making graphic his desire to have chords held through each other on the piano with the damper pedal is to be seen in measure fifteen. The piano part shows four whole-note chords following each other, but the vocal line shows that these chords are to be sounded with the time of no more than a half note between them, and that they are then to be held through each other for the extra period of time.

The reason for the particular deployment of musical forces in this song derives from the words. Browning's poem turns about the attempt of man to take unto himself the glory of God. There follows the despair of finding this futile; then comes the realization of error and an understanding of love that takes precedence over power. The last line reads: 'And with much power, always, always much more love,' as the strands of the music come gently together.

The Second Pianoforte Sonata 'Concord, Mass., 1840–1860'

Each movement of the Second Piano Sonata bears one of the names that made the village of Concord, Massachusetts, famous during the mid-nineteenth century. The first — *Emerson* — is the substantial sonata-form movement; next comes *Hawthorne,* a fantastic scherzo. The third movement bears the name of *The Alcotts;* it is simple and religious. The last movement, *Thoreau,* is a kind of mystic reflection on man's identification of himself with nature.

Toward the end of the epilogue in *Essays Before a Sonata* Ives has inserted a footnote:

. . . the first movement (Emerson) of the music which

is the cause of all these words, was first thought of in terms of a large orchestra or a piano concerto, the second (Hawthorne) in terms of a piano or a dozen pianos, the third (Alcotts) of an organ (or piano with voice or violin), and the last (Thoreau) in terms of strings, colored possibly with a flute or horn.

The Sonata is built on two motifs. One, epic in nature, consists of three repeated notes and a drop of a third to the fourth note — in other words, the opening motif of Beethoven's Fifth Symphony. Ives's 'second' motif (actually it is heard before the other one) is lyric in nature and moves mostly in conjunct motion.

The two motifs are exposed immediately. The first five bass notes give the lyric motif (Ex. 17), and an inverted

Ex. 17. From *Concord Sonata*.

form is used contrapuntally in contrary motion in the treble; a few beats later the soprano part begins a series of dotted eighth notes with underlying sixteenth-note pulses. The first accented note, C, has three such pulses; its drop to G-sharp gives the first suggestion of the epic motif (Ex. 18). This is immediately followed by three accented E's

Ex. 18. From *Concord Sonata*.

dropping to C-sharp, and then come three accented D-sharps in the bass that drop to C. The scheme is atonal, the theme arriving at the C-sharp in the middle but starting from and concluding with C-natural. One therefore goes as far afield as possible at once, but is returned promptly to the starting point. This becomes important later on, for in the final form at the very end of the Sonata, the three typical repeated notes are followed, not by the drop of a third, but by the same note over again, for a fourth time, thus resolving everything into unity.

In the initial exposition of the epic motif many varieties and permutations of the lyric motif are used against it in several-part polyphony. When the epic motif arrives triumphantly on the low C, this note is given a bar line to mark its emphasis. And at this point all the polyphonic strands come to a unison on C also. This is the first bar line in the Sonata, for up to this time there has been no hint of meter.

So in addition to an initial theme, there is a statement of form and idea to open the work, in the sense that all the musical means, melodic line, polyphony, harmonic implications (atonality to tonality), and rhythm, are applied to the materials in such a way as to make obvious the concept of diversity drawing toward unity as its culmination.

It is hard to speak of the themes formed by an extension of the motifs as first or second themes, because although the 'first,' or epic, theme is more noticeable and is nearer in character to most sonata 'first' themes, actually the lyric theme is heard earlier, and there is usually some interweaving of the two whenever they appear. They both come in and out, each time in a new form, through all four movements. Their simplest form is not that of the initial exposition, of course. Example 19 shows simple forms of the epic theme; example 20, the lyric one.

Ives himself names the contrasting sections of the *Emer-*

Ex. 19. From *Concord Sonata*.

Ex. 20. From *Concord Sonata*.

son movement *prose* (the first section) and *verse* (the second). The latter is simple and more metrical and repetitious in structure. Both motifs appear freely in both sections, but the epic motif comes in oftener in the prose sections. The longest verse section (starting on p. 8 of the Arrow Press edition) develops the lyric theme from its simplest form in the first measure through a series of greater and greater leaps until one reaches the fantastic four-octave jump in the ninth measure (Ex. 21). It is noteworthy that

Ex. 21. From *Concord Sonata*.

the listener does not have the difficulty he might expect in following these leaps. Because the distances are widened gradually, and because the relations of the tones to appear in different octaves have first been heard within a single octave, and with the help of the ostinato bass harmonic figure that glues the whole thing together, most auditors not only have no trouble following the large intervals, but have been inclined to pick this passage for special admiration.

Almost every conceivable type of variation is applied to

the epic motif. It appears first in dotted eighth notes, then in quarters, eighths, sixteenths, halves, whole notes, and dotted halves. The last interval is sometimes a major, sometimes a minor third. There is melodic inversion, with the third going up at the end, and retrograde, both straight and inverted (the third appearing before the three repeated notes). Sometimes, still in connection with the inevitable three repeated tones, the other interval will be shortened to a second, or lengthened to a fifth. Ex. 22 illustrates some of these variations.

Ex. 22. From *Concord Sonata.*

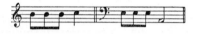

Often several of these developments may appear in contrasting time values against each other polyphonically, usually with elements from the other motif mixed in at the same time. In the development, the fifth note of Beethoven's original motif — the note F, that is to say, that starts the second group (F, F, F, D) — is very important to Ives, and he makes of it an ending note which yet has the embryo of a new starting point within it. The *Emerson* movement ends with the theme G, G, G, E-flat, F and its variation G, G, G, A-flat, G, E-flat, E-flat, F, which is the last note in the tenor. The bass confirms F as an ending tone by a slow A, A, A, F underneath. But there is so much potential activity in the F that it cannot be heard as completely conclusive, and the note becomes a generating point for further activity.

There is, particularly in the prose sections, a constantly running polyphony, often fairly complex. The seeker for the main theme is often aided by accent marks. While there is no indicated meter for prose sections, bar lines are used to mark significant beginning points in the form. The rhythms are varied and contrasting, but not usually wildly hard to grasp or to play, although the appearance is startling because of the way Ives writes whole or half notes only a quarter beat or less apart, as mentioned earlier.

The long verse development (pp. 8–11) is concerned with melodic and harmonic repetitions in flowing style, but three-part polyphony is resumed at once in the next prose section (p. 12). Following this, first one theme and then the other is developed in increasingly short sections (until p. 15), from which point, starting broadly and slowly on the epic motif and moderately and easily on the verse motif, there are two pages of gradually increasing motion and force up to the climactic recapitulation, fortissimo, of the epic motif (p. 18). This is marked *faster*. The long leading passage points up the starkness of the famous notes, now heard repeated several times in Beethoven's key and in rhythmic unison for the first time. The music ebbs from this climax in a regular 4/2 meter that is carried rather ponderously by the bass; everything is softer and slower, until at the end of the movement the tenor and bass have an interwoven form of the epic theme, with tiny high overtone-like, faint-sounding thirds — the minor thirds that are one facet of the epic motif — moving against the major thirds that are being dealt with in the lower instruments.

As is the case with all well-constructed sonatas, all the materials out of which the whole of the rest of the work is to be built can be found in the first measure of the *Concord Sonata*. The rhythmic and thematic development is more involved than in classic examples, but it is of the same general sort, of course, with the important exception that it does not proceed from the simple to the complex, but the reverse.

The *Hawthorne* movement opens with light rapid sixteenths and thirty-seconds, of which Ives remarks that they are not to be taken too literally as exact time values, and with fantastic darting wide melodic leaps and wide horizontal spaces between melody tones. Next comes a section with pre-jazz syncopation against rippling broken chords. Some of this is in consecutive perfect fourths. Since these are rare they give the section a highly original sound; this is followed up later (p. 29) by runs and melodic passages formed of fourths alone.

On page 25 is to be found one of the things that caused great hilarity at Ives's expense in the early 'twenties: all of the keys (black or white) are to be held down without sounding for a distance of 2 octaves plus a second. The idea is to release the dampers on the upper strings so that overtones will be caught by sympathetic vibration, when lower chords and melodies are played. This is very effective, producing a swirl of sound rather like echoes within a cave. But the appearance of a piece of wood on the piano keys was more than baffling to conventional recital audiences: they resented it so actively that they remained quite deaf to the fine sound.

About the middle of the movement the epic motif comes in definitely, in keeping with the character of the *Hawthorne* idea, in a syncopated version (Ex. 23). Although

Ex. 23. From *Concord Sonata.*

the syncopation is very discreet, the idea of 'syncopating Beethoven' came in for a lot of abuse, along with 'playing the piano with a board.'

The middle section has frequent change of pace; it is

followed by short sections, each introducing a new aspect of the fundamental theme. Then there is a return to the very fast tempo of the beginning. The original syncopated section was based on groups of four sixteenth notes. The syncopation often turned them into actual groups of three sixteenths, with off-beat accenting. The final section, in recapitulating this idea, abandons the syncope and has a basic figure of three sixteenths which changes the basic dance form from minstrel show style to jig style. This part rises to a fortissimo, finally landing unexpectedly on the Beethoven motif.

During the first two movements a great deal has been going on all the time: many polyphonic strands, complex chords and polychords, and rhythmical irregularities. There are only momentary suggestions of an underlying key. In the third movement (*The Alcotts*) this many-sided activity changes to a wholehearted simplicity. The opening (Ex. 24) presents the epic motif in lyric form, simply harmo-

Ex. 24. From *Concord Sonata*.

nized, with all the parts in one key. The rhythm is as uninvolved as a hymn, and indeed, the spirit of this movement derives from the contained religion of the family church, and the domestic music of daughters playing the piano in the parlor.

In the second measure key signatures are introduced for the first time in the Sonata. Polytonality is indicated: the right hand has two flats — which may well be a mistake, as there seems to be no reason for not using three flats, since the keys involved certainly seem to be E-flat major and C minor. And the left hand has four flats: A-flat major, with nothing but tonic and dominant chords in this part throughout. Far from seeming involved, this duality of closely-related keys, with the constant tonic on A-flat and the modulations through easy dominant sevenths that combine with it, from E-flat to C minor and back again, all sounds calm and simple, very different from the constant flurry and change of the earlier movements.

In the course of this section the epic theme is stated and then extended as in Example 25. A second section, no longer

Ex. 25. From *Concord Sonata*.

with key signature, develops both the motifs and lengthens them, using plain chords and key changes, and finally arrives at the dominant seventh chord of E-flat major. Here for the first time there is introduced a single key signature (three flats) in all the parts, and 4/4 meter. There is a longer melody formed of snatches of four different familiar tunes, including *Loch Lomond* and the *Wedding March* from Lohengrin, all simply harmonized. This melody modulates to the dominant; after ten measures it returns to the original tonic and repeats. This middle section is then broken up by a 4½/4 measure leading to a development of the lyric theme in two-part, note-against-note counterpoint, finally arriving at the epic theme as a coda. This coda thunders in C major, but at the very end, just when one feels that this is bound to be a really final ending, the melody arrives at a B-flat — and the final cadence is a B-flat chord that leads to a C major chord. This is the closest to modal usage that is to be found in Ives's music. But although it suggests a mixolydian cadence, one cannot escape the conclusion that the composer means it to suggest that the theme is still unfinished, and that just when one thinks one has arrived at the end, a new key is in the offing with new and tempting possibilities.

The final movement, *Thoreau,* is very slow in tempo but subject to sudden darting runs. They include, in the first line, what is surely the only appearance in music of 1024th notes. This only a playful Ivesian way of saying: 'Play as fast as you are able!' There are frequent ritardandi and accellerandi. The mood is contemplative, with an inner calm that defies the seeming capricious lack of order with which all sorts of materials from other movements are recapitulated. The apparent chaos acts as a long, powerful leading force toward the denouement, in which the Sonata's epic and lyric themes are blended in one long melody. This ends finally on the three repeated notes of the epic motif, not now followed by the final note that one anticipates. For this melody Ives suddenly calls for a flute, although there has been no hint until now that this is anything but a piano sonata. (There is an alternative passage for piano alone in case the pianist has no flute handy!) Before the 'flute' passage is finished, there begins an ostinato in the bass that lasts to the final cadence. This is the musical representation of a philosophical concept that Ives has reserved for the close of the work.

One recalls that in Beethoven's original motif there is a descending major third, then a descending minor third, then a third that arrives at the tonic a fifth below the initial note. It suggests a minor triad. Beethoven kept the upgoing version — a major third up, followed by a minor third up, leading to the fifth above, this time implying a major triad, for the main theme of the last movement.

Ives's final ostinato, which also emphasizes upgoing aspects of this motif, suggests simultaneous minor and major thirds (Ex. 26), A to C to C-sharp; on top of the C-sharp

Ex. 26. From *Concord Sonata.*

there is G, a fifth up, with its major third, B. Here are all the immediate implications of the epic motif in ascending form. For the final few notes (Ex. 27) the low A goes to C while

Ex. 27. From *Concord Sonata.*

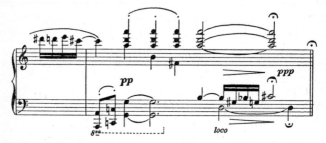

the C-sharp is sounding above, thus fulfilling the combined major-minor implications of the bass ostinato that has sounded so many times with the C and C-sharp in succession instead of together.

For the final cadence the epic motif appears on the tonic and dominant triads; but Ives concludes it — and this is the culmination of the whole work — on the identical pitch: at last it refuses either to rise or fall but is completed where it stands.

Underneath this, there is the impression of both a plagal

cadence (G to D in the bass) and an authentic cadence (the low A, part of the dominant chord A, C-sharp, E to begin with, is heard to ascend to the final D). Just when one supposes that all possible dualities have been led into the final unison, however, the tenor part ends with a hint of the epic motif on the leading tone.

And never has the leading tone been fraught with so many implications. It will obviously resolve to the upper tonic eventually, and it now leads toward this point with yearning and intensity. But one is inescapably led to the realization that this suggestion of simultaneous tonic and dominant chords has only opened a new cycle of duality on a new plane of musico-philosophical existence. As the Sonata concludes, one senses that the ending is not final and that the music will continue to sound in the imagination and to grow.

Universe Symphony

This work seems never to have proceeded beyond the planning-and-sketch stage. Several different orchestras, with huge conclaves of singing men and women, are to be placed about in valleys, on hillsides, and on mountain tops. Ives described its genesis in his autobiographical notes:

When we were in the Keene Valley, on the Plateau, in 1915, with Edie, I started something that I had had in mind for some time: trying out a parallel way of listening to music suggested by looking at a view.

First, with the eyes toward the sky or tops of the trees, taking the earth or foreground subjectively (that is, not focussing the eye on it), and then

Second, looking at the earth and land and seeing the sky and the top of the foreground subjectively.

In other words, giving a musical piece in two parts,

but both played at the same time . . . the whole played through twice, first when the listener focusses his ears on the lower or Earth music, and the next time on the upper, or Heavens music . . .

The Earth part is represented by lines, starting at different points and at different intervals. A kind of uneven and interlapping counterpoint, sometimes reaching nine or ten different lines representing the ledges, rocks, woods and land formations, lines of trees and forest, meadows, roads, rivers, and undulating lines of mountains in the distance, that you catch in a wide landscape. And with this counterpoint, a few of the instruments playing the melodic lines are put into a group, playing masses of chords built around intervals, in each line. This is to represent the body of the earth, where the rocks, trees and mountains arise. Between the lower group and the upper, there is a vacant space of four tones between B-natural and E-natural.

The part of the orchestra representing the Heavens has its own chord system, but its counterpoint is chordal . . . There are three groups in some places divided into four or five. On the lower corner of the second page of the sketch, this chordal counterpoint is broken by long chords, but stays this way for only a short time. These two main groups come into relation harmonically only in cycles, that is, they go around their own orbit and come to meet each other only where their circles eclipse.

Ives went on to say that he might 'expand this into a larger work than originally intended,' and then in 1936 or 1937, a good many years after the description above, he wrote on the back of a page of this 'old manuscript' the following:

Plan for a Universe Symphony

1. Formation of the countries and mountains
2. Evolution in nature and humanity
3. The rise of all to the spiritual

This is the last large work that Charles Ives has worked on. It is unfinished and intentionally so, as it is the culminating expression of his 'music of the Idea,' so gigantic, so inclusive, and so exalted that he feels no one man could ever complete it; anyone else may add to it if he cares to do so, and the collaboration of more than one composer friend, the writer among them, has been invited. That such collaboration has not yet seemed possible is not a disappointment, for the full expression of the universe in sound is something sure to come about when growth and freedom have created men able to encompass it.

APPENDIX

A List of the Compositions

of Charles Edward Ives

This list of compositions is conceived as a part of the composer's biography, intended first of all to record details of his relation to his music. The list is chronological in order to show, as nearly as available evidence now allows, what music Ives had on his mind in a given year. The compiler's starting point was a typewritten list of his works made up and distributed occasionally by the composer himself in the middle 'thirties — a list that exists in three slightly variant forms. Ives has said that no one of these is completely accurate, but he has never been much interested in further correction, although the sight of an error in print has sometimes spurred him to momentary concern about 'getting things *right!*' His lists simply represent his best guess about his music at a given time. Two sets of dates exist for several works, both given by Ives himself; three or four dates, frankly guesses, have been contributed by the compiler (in brackets). There are a few exceptions here to the conventional listing of a work under the latest year mentioned for it by the composer, usually due to his having offered more than one possibility, so that the compiler was forced to make a choice. Tempo marks were used by Ives on one list as titles for a number of chamber works, but this produced so many LARGOS and PRESTOS that they could only be distinguished by using their descriptive subtitles. The list below follows the example of several publishers in using Ives's subtitle as the primary identification; tempo marks are included chiefly where they can be helpful in sorting out pieces about which there has been confusion.

Every song known to us is listed here, although many of them are very short, because so many instrumental pieces became songs and so many songs were turned into instrumental music that Ives's work as a composer is incomprehensible without them.

Ives often lists his instrumentation in an unconventional order, and whenever available to us his listing has been kept, as evidence of an instrumental perspective in the composer's mind. Some of the versions he lists have not been found, and although the list below follows the instrumentation that Ives has given, the published or recorded versions are often different. It seems likely that some of Ives's instrumentations are suggestions to himself for the future, never realized. On the other hand, a more thorough search through cabinets and the West Redding barn may turn up scores in the exact form he has listed for them. At present this is impossible to determine.

Ives has sometimes played on the word SET, which may mean a group of pieces more or less like a suite; or a musical setting of a text; or a setting (i.e. a sitting-down-together of players) for a specified number of people; or, finally, a specified setting of instruments, as it might be a place setting — knife, fork and spoon — at table. Or he may mean any two of these at once, or all of them. Three pieces on Ives's list, written at about the same time and for approximately the same group of instruments, were bracketed by him with the information that they may be played together or separately, and so the compiler has ventured to give the group a name: SET for string quartet, 'basso' and piano. 'Basso' is in quotes because Ives plays on the word: in one piece it means a male singer, in the second a solo on a bass instrument with additional string bass ad lib., and in the third piece there is an important bass line for the cello (duplicated in the piano part).

The contents of eleven bound volumes of photostat copies of manuscript sheets of Ives's music, now at the American Music Center in New York, nine similar ones at the Music Division of the New York Public Library (42nd Street), and four others at the Library of Congress, all marked CHAMBER MUSIC, have been examined to supplement Ives's entries. Some of the bound volumes include a few pages of holograph sketches (in photostat reproduction of course), but the legible copies are practically always in another hand, by copyists Price or Hanke, as Ives seems to have given up the making of fair copies of his music himself at a fairly early date.

At various times Ives had several sets of these volumes of photostat manuscript sheets bound in brown cloth, to give to libraries, publishers, performers, and friends. No two sets seem to contain the same number of volumes, and although the volumes are numbered serially, volumes of different sets numbered identically do not always have identical contents. Galley proofs of a work have found their way into at least one of them. Such volumes were conceived only as a convenience to the composer and the recipient, not as a publication project.

Brief mention of publishers and recording companies has been included to guide inquirers. No distinction is made between works in print, on rental, or under contract to appear.

The Arrow Press and New Music Editions may be addressed care of the American Music Center, 250 West 57th Street, New York; Mercury Music Corporation, 47 West 63rd Street, New York; Bomart Music Publications, Inc., Hillsdale, N.Y.; Peer International or Southern Music Publishers, Inc., 1619 Broadway, New York. Carl Fischer, 56 Cooper Square, New York, now handles the FIRST ORCHESTRAL SET: *Three Places in New England,* originally published by Birchard.

CH stands for Concert Hall, a record subscription society. SPA is the Society of Participating Artists. *NMQR* stands for *New Music Quarterly Recordings* or *New Music Recordings.*

Any further inquiry should be addressed to The American Composers Alliance, 250 West 57th Street, New York.

Published Song Collections

114 SONGS, 1884–1921. Privately printed, 1922; reprinted [1925?]. Out of print. The small arabic numbers following titles in the list below give the serial number of the song in this collection and in the collection called 50 SONGS as well, q.v.

50 SONGS, 1891–1921. Privately printed, 1923. Contains 51 songs. Plates from the 114 SONGS were used without correcting serial or page numbers, so that the same songs have the same numbers in both volumes; if a song was omitted in the smaller volume, its serial and page numbers are missing too. Titles selected by the composer for this collection are starred in the list below.

7 SONGS, 1902–1921. Cos Cob-Arrow Press, 1932. Nos. 2, 10, 14, 23, 29, 42, 67, reprinted from the 114 SONGS.

34 SONGS, 1889–1921. Publ. by *New Music,* VII–1, 1933–34. Three of
these had not appeared before: AT PARTING, 1889; SOLILO-
QUY, 1907; SONG FOR HARVEST SEASON, 1894. The remaining 31 titles were reprinted from the 114 SONGS: Nos. 3, 4, 5, 6,
8, 9, 18, 19, 20, 21, 24, 25, 26, 27, 31, 36, 37, 39, 45, 48, 57, 59, 69,
73, 74, 83, 97, 103, 105, 107, 113.

18 (19) SONGS, 1894, 1925. Publ. by *New Music,* IX–1, 1935. Five of
these songs had not appeared before: AESCHYLUS AND SOPHO-
CLES, 1922; A FAREWELL TO LAND, 1925; GENERAL WIL-
LIAM BOOTH ENTERS HEAVEN, 1914; ON THE ANTIP-
ODES, 1915 and 1923; REQUIEM, Nov. 1911. The remaining
14 titles were reprinted from the 114 SONGS: 1, 13, 22, 30, 33, 34,
40, 51, 72, 82, 84, 100, 104, 111. The original title of this collection
was 18 SONGS, but this was changed to 19 SONGS after the first
edition, when the editor got around to counting the songs actually
in the volume.

4 SONGS, 1901, 1921. Publ. by Mercury, 1953. Nos. 9, 21, 22, 78, reprinted from the 114 SONGS.

10 SONGS, 1888–1902. Publ. by Peer, 1954. Nos. 56, 70, 75, 86, 99, 102,
106, 110, 112, 114, reprinted from the 114 SONGS. Texts for Nos. 1,
3 and 6 of this collection are by the composer, not by Mrs. Ives.

12 SONGS, 1894–1921. Publ. by Peer, 1954. Nos. 7, 12, 15, 16, 32, 35,
62, 65, 76, 91, 101, 109, reprinted from the 114 SONGS.

Chronological List † of Compositions

1888   SLOW MARCH[114], text by CEI. 'To the Children's Faithful
Friend' [the family dog]. Quotes *Dead March* from SAUL.

1889   AT PARTING, text by Peterson. *In* 34 SONGS. SPA recording.

† Authors of the texts of the songs follow the titles; they appear as
given by the composer in the early publications, or by Mrs. Ives in 1954.
CEI is of course Charles Edward Ives; HTI is Harmony Twichell Ives,
his wife.

The small figures following each song title correspond to its serial number in 114 SONGS; titles reprinted in 50 SONGS are starred. A small °
indicates that the composer has listed the piece as 'no good.'

The last two song collections, above, appeared too late for mention in
individual entries on this list.

TURN YE, TURN YE. Publ. by Mercury. For SATB with piano or organ.

1891 VARIATIONS ON A NATIONAL HYMN [*America*]. Publ. by Mercury. For organ. Introduction, chorale and five variations, with bi-tonal interludes added later, sometime before 1894. This is the earliest surviving piece using polytonality.

ADESTE FIDELES, a prelude. Publ. by Mercury. For organ.

WHEN STARS ARE IN THE QUIET SKIES[113]*, text by Bulwer-Lytton. SPA recording.

1892 A SONG — *for anything*[89]°, CEI.

TO EDITH[112]*, HTI. The poem was written for Edith Ives, after 1910, to fit earlier music.

[1893] THE WORLD'S HIGHWAY[90]°, HTI. Text much later than music.

[1894] FUGUE IN FOUR KEYS. Written as an exercise and shown to his father sometime before entering Yale, possibly as early as 1891 or 1892.

1894 CIRCUS BAND, a quickstep[56]*, CEI. Publ. by Peer; CH recording (voice and piano). For SSATTBB, 3 woodwinds, 3 trombones, tuba, violins, cello, bass drums and piano; piano part missing, not written into score. Fragments and parodies of college songs.

CANON[111], Moore.

KAREN[91]*, 'author unknown to composer.'

SONG FOR HARVEST SEASON, text from an old hymn. *In* 34 SONGS. For voice, cornet, trombone and 'basso' (instrumental); or voice and organ.

1895 FUGUES, 1892–1895. For organ and strings. So listed by Ives; possibly a bound collection of photostats, but not located.

INTERCOLLEGIATE MARCH°, for military band. Pepper

& Co., Phila., *c.* 1895. The first music by Ives to appear in print. No score located; parts for small orchestra [arr. B. Herrmann?] are in CBS library.

A NIGHT SONG[88], Moore. CH recording. Small orchestra, 1943, arr. Amedeo de Filippi.

A NIGHT THOUGHT[107]*, Moore. SPA recording.

A SON OF A GAMBOLIER[54], 'traditional.' For voice and piano, then 2 pages of piano solo, then final page adds melody — first for kazoos, then piccolos, ocarinas, and fifes.

SONGS MY MOTHER TAUGHT ME[108]*, Heyduk, trans.

WALTZ[109], CEI.

THE WORLD'S WANDERERS[110]*, Shelley.

1896   STRING QUARTET No. 1, *A Revival Service*. Publ. by Peer.
       I Prelude: Allegro
      II Offertory: Adagio cantabile, 'from an organ prelude played in 1898.'
     III Postlude: Allegro marziale — Andante con moto — Allegro marziale, 'played in Centre Church, New Haven, 1896. Another movement opened this work originally, 'a kind of a choral prelude, and used in part of SYMPHONY No. 3.'

AMPHION[106]*, Tennyson.

FOR YOU AND ME°, No. 966 in Molineux' Collection of Part Songs and Choruses for male voices, *c.* 1896 by Geo. Molineux, New York City. Ives remembers nothing about this publication but says (1953), 'It was not a good song.'

IN THE ALLEY[53]°, CEI.

MARIE[92]*, Gottschall.

AN OLD FLAME[87]°, CEI.

WILLIAM WILL, text by S. B. Hill, a Danbury lady. Willis Woodward & Co., N.Y. A McKinley campaign song.

1897 DREAMS[85°], Porteous (trans).

MEMORIES[102], CEI.

MY NATIVE LAND[101], 'traditional.'

1898 SYMPHONY No. 1 in D minor. Sketches begun 1896; scoring begun Aug. 1897, finished May 1898. Publ. by Peer. For symphony orchestra.
  I Allegro moderato
  II Adagio molto, sostenuto
  III Scherzo — Vivace
  IV Allegro molto

FORWARD INTO LIGHT[99]. Text by Alford from St. Bernard. Aria for tenor or soprano from a cantata THE CELESTIAL COUNTRY, 1898–1899.

PSALM SIXTY-SEVEN. Publ. by Arrow; Columbia recording (out of print). For SATB.

ROSAMUNDE[79], Bélanger.

Harvest Home, I of THREE HARVEST HOME CHORALES, 1898–1912.

1899 THE CELESTIAL COUNTRY, a cantata, 1898–1899. Text by Alford from St. Bernard. Publ. by Peer. Mixed chorus, quartet, soli, strings, brass and organ.

ICH GROLLE NICHT[83], Heine. SPA recording.

NAUGHT THAT COUNTRY NEEDETH[98]*. Text by Alford from St. Bernard. Aria for baritone from a cantata, THE CELESTIAL COUNTRY, 1898–1899.

NIGHT OF FROST IN MAY[84]*, Meredith. CH recording.

THE SOUTH WIND[97]*, HTI.

1900 PRELUDE. Fragment [before 1900] from a pre-PRE-FIRST SONATA for violin and piano.

A CHRISTMAS CAROL[100]*, [before 1900], 'traditional.'

ALLEGRO[95], HTI.

BERCEUSE[93]*, CEI.

IN SUMMER FIELDS[82]*, Almers. Date in 18 (19) SONGS is 1898.

NINETY-SIX or ROMANZO DI CENTRAL PARK[96]°, Hunt.

THE OLD MOTHER[81], Vinje.

OMENS AND ORACLES[86]°, 'author unknown to composer.'

WHERE THE EAGLE[94], Turnbull.

1901 ALLEGRO. 'Started as a FIRST VIOLIN SONATA and not completed.' This and the LARGO for violin, clarinet and piano, 1902, are what remain from the PRE-FIRST SONATA for violin and piano. May prove to be part of TRIO for violin, clarinet and piano, 1902–1903, not located.

LET THERE BE LIGHT, a prelude, CEI. Publ. by Peer. Processional for male chorus or trombones, organ, and an extra organ player or four violins. 'To the choir of the Central Presbyterian Church, Dec. 1901.'

FROM THE STEEPLES or FROM THE STEEPLES AND THE MOUNTAINS. For two sets of [church] bells [i.e. chimes], each with a high and low part (piano may be substituted), trumpet and trombone.

Two organ pieces that turned into I and III of SYMPHONY No. 3, 1901–1904.

CHANSON DE FLORIAN[78], J. P. Claris, Chevalier de Florian.

THE CHILDREN'S HOUR[74]*, Longfellow, CH recording.

ELEGIE[77]*, Gallet.

I TRAVELLED AMONG UNKNOWN MEN[75]*, Wordsworth.

QU'IL M'IRAIT BIEN[76], 'author unknown to composer.'

1902 THE ALL-ENDURING [before 1902]. Publ. by Mercury. For voice and piano.

ANTHEMS, BRASS BAND PIECES and MARCHES, PIECES FOR THEATRE ORCHESTRA, and some DANCE MUSIC, 1886–1902. So listed by Ives, but probably never bound in a single volume.

ORGAN MUSIC, 1896–1902. For church service and recital. So listed by Ives. Possibly a bound collection of photostats, but not located.

OVERTURES, 1901–1902. 'For large and small orchestras. Mostly incomplete; parts used elsewhere.' So listed by Ives; probably never bound in a single volume.

SYMPHONY No. 2, 1897–1902. Publ. by Southern; SPA recording. For symphony orchestra.

    I Andante moderato, 'from an organ sonata played in part at Centre Church.'

    II Allegro (scored August 1900).

    III Adagio cantabile. 'Organ prelude, Centre Church, 1896. Scored 1902. Copied with slight revision, 1909.'

    IV Lento maestoso.

    V Allegro molto vivace. 'Partly from an early overture AMERICAN WOODS (*Brookfield*). The part suggesting a Steve Foster tune, while over it the old farmers fiddled a barn dance with all of its jigs, gallops and reels, was played in Danbury on the old Wooster House Bandstand in 1889 . . . Slow movement [III or IV?] was replaced by another in 1909 or 1910.'

LARGO, 1901–1902. Publ. by Southern; EMS-Polymusic recording. For violin, clarinet and piano. Originally for violin and organ (solo stop), then part of the PRE-FIRST SONATA for violin and piano, 1901, and finally for clarinet trio as above. *See* ALLEGRO, 1901. May prove to be part of TRIO for violin, clarinet and piano, 1902–1903, not located.

HARPALUS, *an ancient pastoral*[73], text from Percy's *Reliques*. CH recording.

ILMENAU: OVER ALL THE TREETOPS[68]*, Goethe (transl. HTI).

MIRAGE[70]*, C. G. Rossetti. CH recording.

ROUGH WIND[69], Shelley. 'From an orchestral score.' CH recording.

SLUGGING A VAMPIRE[72]. See TARRANT MOSS[72], 1902.

TARRANT MOSS[72], music for a text by Kipling of which only the first four words are quoted. Published in 18 (19) SONGS as SLUGGING A VAMPIRE with a second text by CEI. 'This was originally to Kipling's TARRANT MOSS but as copyright permission was not obtained the nice poetry about Hearst was written (not by Mr. Kipling).'

THERE IS A LANE[71]*, [HTI].

WALKING[67], CEI.

WEIL AUF MIR[80], Lenau.

1903 TRIO for violin, clarinet and piano, 1902–1903. Listed by Ives but not located. *See* ALLEGRO, 1901, and LARGO, 1902.

SCHERZO, II of SET for string quartet, 'basso' and piano, 1903–1914.

1904 SPRING SONG[65]*°, HTI.

HYMN[20]*, I of SET for string quartet, 'basso' and piano, 1903–1914.

Thanksgiving and/or Forefathers' Day, IV of A SYMPHONY: HOLIDAYS, 1904–1913.

SYMPHONY No. 3, 1901–1904. Publ. by Arrow; Station WCFM recording. For symphony orchestra.
> I Andante maestoso. From an organ piece, 1901; recopied with slight revision, 1911. Ends with old hymn *Take It to the Lord.*
> II Allegro. Concluding march theme is the Welsh battle song known in the United States as *All Through the Night.*
> III Largo. From an organ piece, 1901.

GENERAL SLOCUM, *July, 1904.* Fragmentary sketches for a boat disaster piece — suggestions for pre-explosion and explosion instrumentation: what Ives calls a 'take-off.'

AUTUMN LANDSCAPE FROM PINE MOUNTAIN. Fragmentary sketches for strings, woodwinds, and cornet.

THE LIGHT THAT IS FELT[66]*, Whittier. Publ. by Mercury.

1905 Two movements of a PRE-SECOND STRING QUARTET. 'Started as a SECOND STRING QUARTET; uncomplete parts used in later pieces for orchestra.' Ives refers to this piece as the FIRST STRING QUARTET or the SECOND STRING QUARTET depending on whether he remembers the one he called *A Revival Service* (STRING QUARTET No. 1, 1896); ultimately he abandoned it. A third movement that had originally belonged to this PRE-SECOND STRING QUARTET was apparently appropriated for part of SYMPHONY No. 3, 1901–1904 — probably when the latter was recopied in 1911.

THREE-PAGE SONATA for piano, Saranac Lake, August 1905. Publ. by Mercury. A burlesque of sonata form. Manuscript was three pages long, hence the title.

1906 THE POND. Published as II of THREE OUTDOOR SCENES, 1906–1911. For strings, flute and voice or English horn, harp, [church] bells [i.e. chimes] or celesta or piano.

THE CAGE[64], CEI, adapted 1906 for voice and piano from I of SET for theatre or chamber orchestra, 1904–1911.
In the Night, III of SET for theatre or chamber orchestra, 1904–1911.

1907 CALCIUM LIGHT NIGHT, 1898–1907. Publ. by *New Music* XXVI-4, 1953. Published in Ives's original version for chamber orchestra. Version arr. by HC, bound in volume of Ives's chamber music at the N.Y. Public Library, is a simplification Ives asked HC to make about 1933, 'putting some of the harder string parts in a second piano and easing up on some of the other players.'

CENTRAL PARK IN THE DARK, 1898–1907. Publ. by Bomart; EMS-Polymusic recording. For chamber orchestra; published as III of THREE OUTDOOR SCENES. Might be played with CALCIUM LIGHT NIGHT, 1898–1907, with which it was originally paired by Ives among several 'cartoons or take-offs of undergraduate and other events, academic, anthropic [sic], urban, athletic and tragic.'

YALE-PRINCETON GAME, August 1907. The wedge-formation piece: notes set on paper like men on the football field — one note runs around left end for a loss, etc. Includes kazoos. Incomplete; a sketch for a 'take-off.'

GIANTS vs. CUBS, August 1907. Another sketch for a 'take-off,' this time a baseball game.

SPACE AND DURATION. Sketches, incomplete, for string quartet and a mechanical piano if desired. Based on the sequence 2, 3, 5, 7, 11, 7, 5, 3, 2. 'Seemed far-fetched at the time but doesn't now (1932).'

SOLILOQUY, CEI. *In* 34 SONGS. 'A study in sevenths and other things'; 'a take-off of the Yankee drawl.'

THOSE EVENING BELLS[63], Moore.

1908   ALL THE WAY AROUND AND BACK (before 1908). Publ. by Peer. A scherzo for piano (one or two players), violin or flute, flute or clarinet, bugle or trumpet, bells or French horn.

SOME SOUTHPAW PITCHING for piano (before 1908). Publ. by Mercury.

THE UNANSWERED QUESTION, *a cosmic landscape* (before June 1908). Publ. *in* Boletín Latino-Americano de Música V, Oct. 1941 and also by Southern; EMS-Polymusic recording. Largo and presto. For trumpet and four flutes, treble woodwinds, and string orchestra.

SONATA NO. 1 for violin and piano, 1903–1908 (or 1902–1910). Publ. by Peer; Lyrichord recording.
    I Andante — Allegro
    II Largo
    III Allegro — Andante cantabile (quotes old hymn: *Watchman, Tell Us of the Night*) — Allegro primo.

THE ANTI-ABOLITIONIST RIOTS for piano (about 1908).

Publ. by Mercury. Originally further described as 'in Boston in the 50's.' After publication Ives realized he was mistaken in the time and place and that it should have read 'in Philadelphia in the 40's.' Moreover, his grandfather was an ardent Abolitionist, not an anti-Abolitionist as stated in the note. So the first edition was withdrawn and corrected.

THE INNATE[40], for string quartet and piano, III of SET for string quartet, 'basso' and piano, 1903–1914. For voice and piano or organ, 1916.

IN RE CON MOTO *et al.* Publ. by Peer. For string quartet and piano. Cross rhythms; some measures of 15/8, 33/8, 11/8, 21/8, 7/4, 33/16.

LARGO RISOLUTO No. 1, *The Law of Diminishing Returns*, [1908]. String quartet and piano.

LARGO RISOLUTO No. 2, *A Shadow Made — a Silhouette*, [1908]. Piano and string quartet.

AUTUMN[60°], HTI.

NATURE'S WAY[61*°], CEI.

THE WAITING SOUL[62°], Cowper.

1909   SONATA No. 1 for piano, 1902–1909. Publ. by Peer; Columbia recording. Ives lists this as a work in seven movements but says only five were copied by photostat. The other two have not been located.

   I Adagio con moto — Andante con moto — Allegro risoluto. Then 'with a certain kind of poise and dignity but not exactly slower,' then 'agitando' followed by 'in a kind of furious way (hit hard!)' and finally 'ease down to Adagio cantabile.'

   II Allegro moderato. First two pages are dated 'Danbury 1902'; then Ives inserts *In the Inn,* as published by *New Music,* arranged from II of SET for theatre or chamber orchestra, 1904–1911. Columbia recording (piano) of *In the Inn.*

   III Largo or Adagio — Allegro — Largo

   IV Andante — Allegro (includes 'a study in "rag" for 5's,

3's and 2's together') — Presto 'as fast as possible.'
V Andante maestoso — Adagio cantabile — Allegro —
Allegro moderato ma con brio.

LIKE A SICK EAGLE[26]*, Keats. Largo molto. An 'intonation'
for English or basset horn, voices in unison ad lib., string
quintet, flute (4 measures) and piano (3 chords); for voice
and piano, 1919–1920.

TOLERANCE[59], a text quoted by Hadley. 'Adapted 1921 to
the above words from a piece for orchestra, 1909.' SPA recording.

Washington's Birthday, re-scored 1913, I of A SYMPHONY:
HOLIDAYS, 1904–1913.

1910 ADAGIO SOSTENUTO [before 1910]. Publ. by Peer. For solo
English or basset horn, flute, violins I, II and III (or viola),
cello ad lib., piano or harp or celesta. 'A song without voice.'

From the INCANTATION[18], Byron, [before 1910]. Allegretto
sombreoso. For solo trumpet or English or basset horn, flute,
3 violins and piano, voice probably ad lib. Originally a 'song
without voice' for English horn, with violins, flutes and
piano. For voice and piano, 1921.

SONATA No. 1 for violin and piano, 1903–1908 or 1902–1910.
See 1908.

SONATA No. 2 for violin and piano, 1903–1910. Publ. by
G. Schirmer; EMS-Polymusic recording. Manuscript first
transcribed by John Kirkpatrick was afterward reworked by
Lou Harrison and then by HC, as CEI continued to think of
further desirable expansion.
   I *Autumn.* Adagio maestoso — Andante con brio. July
   1903–October 1907.
   II *In the Barn.* Alco recording. Presto (in a fast rather
   even quadrille time). Not the same as the Barn Dance
   in *Washington's Birthday,* I of A SYMPHONY:
   HOLIDAYS.
   III *The Revival.* Alco recording. Largo. No relation to
   STRING QUARTET No. 1, *A Revival Service.*

EVIDENCE[58°], CEI.

HIS EXALTATION[46], Robinson. Adapted for voice and piano, 1913, from SONATA No. 2 for violin and piano, 1903–1910.

MISTS[57*], CH recording, HTI.

1911 RAGTIME DANCES, 1900–1911. 'About a dozen, mostly for small theatre orchestra, most used elsewhere; some incomplete.' So listed by Ives; possibly a bound volume of photostats; not located.

SET for theatre or chamber orchestra, or *Theatre Orchestra Set*, 1904–1911. Publ. by *New Music*, OS–5, Jan. 1932, reprinted 1948. Oceanic recording (as THREE PIECES for piano and orchestra, not CEI's title).

    I *In the Cage*, 1906. THE CAGE[64], CEI, for voice and piano, was adapted (1906) from part of this movement and distributed interleaved with the published score.

    II *In the Inn*, 1904–1911. A version of this movement for piano forms part of II of SONATA No. 1 for piano; printed separately and distributed interleaved with the published score. Columbia recording (piano).

    III *In the Night*, 1906. The horn plays a fragment of a minstrel song whose text is included but which is 'unintended to be sung.' NMQR recording (out of print).

THREE OUTDOOR SCENES, 1898–1911. Pub. by Bomart. Not originally so grouped by the composer.

    I HALLOWE'EN, 1911. EMS-Polymusic recording. Allegretto to Presto. For string quartet and piano. 'A kind of an April Fool piece for a Hallowe'en Party.' No connection with A SYMPHONY: HOLIDAYS.

    II THE POND, 1906. For strings, flute, voice or English horn, harp, [church] bells [i.e. chimes] or celesta or piano.

    III CENTRAL PARK IN THE DARK, 1898–1907. EMS-Polymusic recording. For chamber orchestra, 'a cartoon or take-off' that might be paired with CALCIUM LIGHT NIGHT, 1898–1907.

TRIO for violin, cello and piano, 1904–1911. Publ. by Peer.
I Andante moderato.
II Presto — Piu mosso — Adagio — Allegro moderato — Allegro assai — Adagio — Presto. The heading for this movement, TSIAJ, stands for *This Scherzo Is a Joke* (a poor joke, said Ives in 1954).
III Moderato con moto — Andante sostenuto — Maestoso — Andante con moto — Allegro. *Rock of Ages* quoted and varied for 14 measures.

TONE ROADS No. 1, 1911. Publ. by Peer. For chamber orchestra, the 'tone road' here established by cellos and string basses. TONE ROADS Nos. 1, 2, and 3 'not necessarily to be played together.'

BROWNING OVERTURE for symphony orchestra. Publ. by Peer. Four pages of this manuscript were missing and had to be 'recomposed' by Lou Harrison or HC; many places were nearly indecipherable and decisions had to be worked out with the copyist Carl Pagano by the editors — a major detective enterprise which Ives has never since been well enough to confirm except in a general way.

THE LAST READER[3]*, Holmes. Andante con moto or cantabile. For English horn or cornet and voice if desired, at least 4 violins and other strings divisi. Footnote: 'From pieces for two flutes, cornet, violas and organ, 1911.' For voice and piano, 1921. Begins with a quotation from Spohr.

REQUIEM, Nov. 1911, text by Stevenson. *In* 18 (19) SONGS.

SYMPHONY No. 3, 1901–1904, 'recopied with slight revision, 1911.' *See* 1904.

1912 THE GONG ON THE HOOK AND LADDER or FIRE-MEN'S PARADE ON MAIN STREET (sometime before 1912). Publ. by Peer. For chamber orchestra.

THREE HARVEST HOME CHORALES, 1898–1912. Publ. by Mercury, edited by HC. For SATB, brass, string bass and organ.
I *Harvest Home*, 1898, text by Burgess.
II *Lord of the Harvest* (before 1912), text by Gurney.

III *Harvest Home* (before 1912), text by Alford.

TWENTY-TWO for piano [1912]. Publ. by *New Music* XXI–1, 1947. From PIANO PIECES, 1900–1914. The title comes from the number of the page in Ives's music notebook on which this piece was written.

PARACELSUS[30]*, Browning, 1912–1921. 'The first two pages of this are from an overture for orchestra [1911], the last page for the most part was written when this was made into a song later.' Finished 1921.

LINCOLN, THE GREAT COMMONER[11]. Text by Markham. Publ. by *New Music* OS–1, 1932, reprinted as XXVI–2, Jan. 1953. For chorus and large orchestra; for voice and piano, 1921. Meastoso [sic] — Andante — Agitando, con furore — Adagio meastoso.

THE INDIANS[14]*, Sprague. Adagio. A 'song without voice' for English horn, basset horn or trumpet or oboe, bassoon, strings, piano and Indian drum; II of SET for trumpet, saxophone and piano, 1912–1921; for voice and piano, 1921.

THE NEW RIVER[6]*, CEI. Publ. by Peer. For chorus and chamber orchestra; I of SET for trumpet, saxophone and piano, with clarinet and four violins ad lib., 1912–1921; for voice and piano, 1921. 'Parts are different in the score and preferable.'

THE CAMP MEETING[47], Elliot. 'From a movement of SYMPHONY No. 3, 1901–1904.'

Decoration Day, II of A SYMPHONY: HOLIDAYS, 1909–1913.

1913 A SYMPHONY: HOLIDAYS, 1904–1913. 'Recollections of a boy's holidays in a Connecticut country town . . .' 'These movements may be played as separate pieces.' 'These pieces may be lumped together as a symphony.'
    I *Washington's Birthday*, 1909, re-scored in 1913. Publ. by *New Music* OS–20. A part (*Barn Dance*) recorded by

NMQR (out of print). For strings, flute, horn and [church] bells [i.e. chimes], Jew's harps.

II *Decoration Day*, 1912. Publ. by Peer. For large orchestra. Quotes fragments of *Swanee River, Good Night, Ladies, Taps* and the drum roll in the cemetery, then the triumphant march back to town.

III *Fourth of July*, 1912–1913. Publ. by *New Music* OS–3, Adler. For large orchestra. Quotes *Columbia, the Gem of the Ocean*.

IV *Thanksgiving and/or Forefathers' Day*, 1904. Publ. by Peer. For large orchestra and chorus. Ends with a *praise*.

OVER THE PAVEMENTS, 1906–1913. Publ. by Peer; EMS-Polymusic recording. Scherzo for piano, clarinet, bass or saxophone, trumpet and drums; piccolo and three trombones ad lib.

STRING QUARTET No. 2, 1907–1913. Ives's lists have 1903–1910 and 1907–1913; dates for individual movements are on the manuscript in Ives's hand, as below. Publ. by Peer; Disc (Period) recording.

    I *Discussions*, 1911–1913.
    II *Arguments*, 1907.
    III *The Call of the Mountains*, 1911–1913.

DECEMBER[37], da San Geminiano-Rossetti, 1912–1913. Publ. by Peer. For unison male chorus with woodwind and brass; for voice and piano, 1920: 'measures may be marked off to suit the taste.'

THE SEE'R[29], CEI, (before May, 1913). Scherzo for solo cornet, trumpet or French horn, clarinet, alto horn or French horn or trombone or tenor saxophone, piano and drums; for voice and piano, 1920.

HIS EXALTATION[46], Robinson. Adapted for voice and piano, 1913, from SONATA No. 2 for violin and piano, 1903–1910.

WATCHMAN[44]*, Bowring. Adapted for voice and piano, 1913, from SONATA No. 2 for violin and piano, 1903–1910.

1914 SINGLE PIANO PIECES, STUDIES and so on, 1900–1914. So listed by Ives; at least one bound copy of photostats known to exist, but not examined.

THREE PROTESTS FOR PIANO. Publ. by *New Music* XXI–1, 1947. From PIANO PIECES, 1900–1914.
> I March time or faster.
> II 'Adagio or allegro or varied or/and variations, very nice.' Ends with a rest marked F for applause.
> III A canon [once announced but never printed separately].

SONATA No. 3 for violin and piano, 1902–1914. *New Music* XXIV–2, 1951, edited by Sol Babitz and Ingolf Dahl; Lyrichord recording. Ives mentions four movements but this seems to be a mistake.
> I Adagio. A hymn tune with four stanzas and choruses.
> II Allegro. 'This movement was written first for small theatre orchestra in 1902–03 and played in the Globe Theatre, New York, December 1905.'
> III Adagio (cantabile).

SET for string quartet, 'basso' and piano, 1903–1914. Publ. by Peer. Three movements that 'may be played together.'
> I *Hymn*[20*], text from Shutter. Largo cantabile for string quartet and 'basso' (male voice) or solo cello, 1904; for voice and piano, 1921; for string orchestra, 1938 [arr. B. Herrmann?].
> II *Scherzo* for string quartet, 'basso' (string bass) ad lib., 1903. 'Middle section sometime in 1914.'
> III *The Innate*[40], CEI, for string quartet and piano, 1908; for voice and piano or organ, 1916.

ORCHESTRAL SET No. 1 or A NEW ENGLAND SYMPHONY: *Three Places in New England* or *Three New England Places*, 1903–1914. Birchard, 1935; Carl Fischer. For symphony orchestra.
> I *Boston Common*. 'The monument to Colonel Shaw and his colored regiment by St. Gaudens.' Prefatory poem by CEI: 'Moving, marching, faces of souls . . .'
> II *Putnam's Camp*. 'A Revolutionary Memorial Park near Redding Center, Connecticut . . . where the

tune *British Grenadiers* was first adopted by Americans in 1779. A Fourth of July picnic piece.'

III *The Housatonic at Stockbridge*[15], Johnson. Artist (Janssen) recording. For voice and piano, 1921, to fit the text that had suggested the title of the orchestral movement.

DUTY[9-a]*, Emerson (before 1914). For male chorus and orchestra, voices in unison until last 2 measures; for voice and piano, 1921.

GENERAL WILLIAM BOOTH'S ENTRANCE INTO HEAVEN. Text by Vachel Lindsay. *In* 18 (19) SONGS; NMQR recording (out of print). For chorus or solo voice with brass band; arranged for chamber orchestra by John J. Becker, 1934. An expansion of the old Salvation Army hymn: *Are You Washed in the Blood of the Lamb?*

THE RAINBOW or SO MAY IT BE[8], Wordsworth. Publ. by Peer. Andante con spirito. For voice, with strings, flute, harp or piano, celesta and organ, 1914; on another list 'A song without voice' for flute, basset or English horn, strings and piano; for voice and piano, 1921.

1915 SONATA No. 2 for piano (*Concord, Mass. in the 1840's*), 1909–1915. Privately printed, 1919. Publ. by Arrow, 1947, edited by John Kirkpatrick; Columbia recording.

I *Emerson*. 1909–summer, 1912. Begun as a concerto for piano and orchestra but never completed. Later planned as an Emerson Overture, 1909–1911. The published version for piano has retained two measures for viola ad lib. Four different transcriptions of this movement were made by CEI for piano and, like John Kirkpatrick's recorded performance, the version published by Arrow has drawn on all of them, after extensive consultation with the composer.

II *Hawthorne*. Completed 12 Oct. 1915. A scherzo.

III *The Alcotts*. Completed 1915. There was an Alcott or Orchard House Overture (1904) with a theme and some passages used in this piece.

IV *Thoreau*. 1911–1915. As it might be a day with Thoreau alone at Walden Pond, with an echo over the water, and several measures intended to be played by a flute. *See* THOREAU[48] for voice and piano, 1915.

ORCHESTRAL SET No. 2, 1912–1915. Publ. by Peer. For large orchestra.
>   I *An Elegy to Our Forefathers.*
>   II *The Rockstrewn Hills Join in the People's Outdoor Meeting.*
>   III *From Hanover Square North at the End of a Tragic Day (1915), the Voice of the People Again Arose.* Requires a chorus of accordions with soprano concertina in one spot.

SONATA No. 4, *Children's Day at the Camp Meeting,* for violin and piano, 1914–1915. Publ. by Arrow; NMQR recording.
>   I Allegro, in a rather fast march time. Quotes *Wait for the Night Is Coming.*
>   II Largo — Allegro con slugarocko (faster and with action) — Andante — Adagio — Largo.
>   III Allegro. Ends with *Shall We Gather at the River?* In the manuscript the words of this hymn are written under the violin melody, to be followed mentally by the player as a 'song without words unintended to be sung.'

THE MAJORITY or THE MASSES[1], CEI. Listed separately by Ives but not so published. For voice and piano, 1921: 'this is an arrangement in part of a score for orchestra and chorus, 1915. *The Masses* [massed seconds] are a kind of mass-tonal percussion part for different instruments . . .'

TONE ROADS No. 3. Publ. by Peer. For chamber orchestra with 'tone road in chimes or piano . . .' TONE ROADS Nos. 1, 2 and 3 'not necessarily to be played together.'

THOREAU[48], CEI. CH recording. 'Adapted 1915 for voices and piano from themes in a SECOND PIANOFORTE SONATA, 1909–1915.'

THE SWIMMERS[27], Untermeyer. Begun 1915 when poem appeared in the *Yale Review;* finished 1921.

ON THE ANTIPODES, 1915 and 1923. *In* 18 (19) SONGS. For two pianos or organ and string orchestra; for voice and two pianos, 1923.

1916 SYMPHONY No. 4 or SYMPHONY WITH TWO PIANOS or SYMPHONY FOR ORCHESTRA AND PIANOS, 1910–1916, for large orchestra. Movements I and II (*Prelude* and *Scherzo*), publ. by *New Music*, Jan. 1929, with remarks by CEI on a sheet interleaved. The *Prelude* is 'the what and why that the spirit of man asks of Life.' The three subsequent movements are the 'answers in which existence replies.'

> I *Prelude.* Maestoso — adagio. Solo piano with full orchestra. Old hymn tune *Watchman, Tell Us of the Night,* exchanged between muted trumpet and voices or other instruments, ad lib.
> II *Scherzo.* Allegretto. Part of this movement was later arranged by CEI as a fantasy for piano, THE CELESTIAL RAILROAD, [1919?]
> III *Fugue in C major.* Arranged by Bernard Herrmann for radio orchestra; by John Kirkpatrick for piano.
> IV *Finale:* very slowly.

AT THE RIVER[45], Lowry. CH recording; SPA recording. 'A hymn tune from SONATA No. 4, *Children's Day at the Camp Meeting,* for violin and piano, 1914–1915.'

THE INNATE[40], 1908, III of SET for string quartet, 'basso' and piano, 1903–1914; for voice and piano or organ, 1916.

LUCK AND WORK[21], Johnson. Allegro con spirito — Andante. 'From pieces for basset horn, flute, three violins, piano and drums'; for voice and piano, 1920.

1917 A WAR SONG MARCH: THEY ARE THERE! Text by CEI. Publ. by Peer. For unison chorus and symphony orchestra. Enlarged from HE IS THERE! *May 30, 1917*[50]; edited by Lou Harrison.

HE IS THERE! *May 30, 1917*[50], CEI. Second of three songs of the First World War. Quotes *Tenting Tonight* (on a New Camp Ground), the *Battle Cry of Freedom, Marching through Georgia.* Enlarged into A WAR SONG MARCH.

PREMONITIONS[24], Johnson. For voice or unison chorus with small orchestra, 1917; for voice and piano, 1921. 'From pieces for basset horn, flute, strings and piano.'

THE THINGS OUR FATHERS LOVED (*and the greatest of these is Liberty*)[43], CEI.

TOM SAILS AWAY[51], CEI. First of three songs of the First World War.

1919   TONE ROADS No. 2, 1911–1919. Not located.

THE CELESTIAL RAILROAD, a fantasy for piano. Arranged by CEI [1919?] from II of SYMPHONY No. 4, 1910–1916.

AFTERGLOW[39], Cooper.

CRADLE SONG[33]*, text by A. L. Ives (1846). CH recording.

DOWN EAST[55], CEI.

IN FLANDERS FIELDS[49], McRae. Third of three songs of the First World War.

SERENITY[42], Whittier, a unison chant (orch. arr. Amedeo de Filippi, 1943).

1920   SONGS adapted for voice and piano in 1920, from earlier instrumental or choral music:
      DECEMBER[37], da San Geminiano-Rossetti, 1912–1913.
      LIKE A SICK EAGLE[26]*, Keats, 1909.
      LUCK AND WORK[21], Johnson, 1916.

SONGS apparently no earlier than 1920:
      AN ELECTION or IT STRIKES ME THAT or NOVEMBER 2, 1920[22], CEI. For male voice or unison chorus and orchestra, 1920; for voice and piano, 1921.
      AUGUST[35], da San Geminiano-Rossetti.
      THE COLLECTION[38], 'stanzas from old hymns.'
      LA FEDE[34]*, Ariosto.
      GRANTCHESTER[17]*, Brooke.
      MAPLE LEAVES[23], Aldrich.
      OLD HOME DAY[52]*, CEI.

ON THE COUNTER[28c], CEI.

RELIGION[16*], Root as quoted by Bixby.

SEPTEMBER[36], da San Geminiano-Rossetti.

1921　SET for trumpet, saxophone and piano, 1912–1921. Planned by CEI from three songs already in print, the first two composed in 1912, the third in 1921. They were torn from a printed copy of the 114 SONGS and then typewritten headings were added to the printed pages, with a few penciled suggestions in Ives's hand for their instrumentation. Next the pages were copied by photostat and finally they were bound together with the title given above. No score or parts seem to have been made.

  I *The New River*, 1912. For trumpet, clarinet, saxophone, piano, 4 violins ad lib.

  II *The Indians*, 1912. For trumpet, oboe, strings, piano.

  III *Ann Street*, 1921. For trumpet, flute, trombone or baritone horn or baritone saxophone and piano.

SONGS begun earlier and finished in 1921 or adapted in 1921 from earlier instrumental music:

  CHANSON DE FLORIAN[78], J. P. Claris, Chevalier de Florian, 1901.

  DUTY[9-a*], Emerson, (before 1914).

  AN ELECTION or IT STRIKES ME THAT or NOVEMBER 2, 1920[22], CEI, 1920. For voice and piano, 1921.

  THE HOUSATONIC AT STOCKBRIDGE[15], Johnson, 1903–1914.

  HYMN[20*], text quoted by Shutter, 1904.

  from the INCANTATION[18], Byron, before 1910.

  THE INDIANS[14*], Sprague, 1912.

  THE LAST READER[3*], Holmes, 1911.

  LINCOLN, THE GREAT COMMONER[11], CEI, 1912.

  THE MAJORITY or THE MASSES[1], CEI, 1915.

  THE NEW RIVER[6*], CEI, 1912.

  PARACELSUS[30*], Browning, 1912.

  PREMONITIONS[24], Johnson, 1917.

  THE RAINBOW or SO MAY IT BE[8], Wordsworth, 1914.

  TOLERANCE[59], text quoted by Hadley, 1909.

SONGS apparently no earlier than 1921:

AESCHYLUS AND SOPHOCLES, Landor. *In* 18 (19) SONGS. For two male voices with piano and string quartet. Polymodal.

ANN STREET[25], NMQR recording, Morris.

AT SEA[4]*, Johnson. SPA recording.

CHARLIE RUTLAGE[10]*, NMQR recording, text from *Cowboy Songs* [collected by Lomax, 1910]. Ives places this song without a date between two songs composed in 1921.

DISCLOSURE[7]*, CEI.

EVENING[2]*, Milton. NMQR recording.

THE GREATEST MAN[19]*, Collins. NMQR recording.

IMMORTALITY[5]*, CEI.

ONE-TWO-THREE[41], CEI. CH recording.

REMEMBRANCE[12]*, CEI.

RESOLUTION[13]*, CEI. NMQR recording.

THE SIDE SHOW[32], CEI. CH recording.

THE SWIMMERS[27], Untermeyer.

TWO LITTLE FLOWERS[104]*, HTI. NMQR and CH recording.

VITA[9–b]*, Manlius. CH recording.

WALT WHITMAN[31]*, Whitman. SPA recording.

WEST LONDON[105]*, Arnold.

THE WHITE GULLS[103]*, Morris.

1923   ON THE ANTIPODES, CEI. *In* 18 (19) SONGS. For voice or chorus and two pianos. 'A part from 1915.'

1924   THREE QUARTER-TONE PIANO PIECES, 1923–1924. For a 'quarter-tone piano' or two pianos tuned a quarter-tone apart. Another list gives 1903–1904. HC thinks this is an early set of piano pieces to which quarter-tone chords were added at the time CEI helped Hans Barth build his quarter-tone piano about 1924. This would explain the two sets of dates. But as Ives's interest in quarter-tones began in his childhood, the pieces may have had, or at least may have been intended to have, the quarter-tone chords, from the beginning.

I Largo
II Allegro
III Adagio: chorale

1925 A FAREWELL TO LAND, Byron. *In* 18 (19) SONGS. For voice and piano.

1926 ORCHESTRAL SET No. 3, 1919–1926. 'Three movements, one uncomplete.' Not located. Except for the UNIVERSE SYMPHONY, this seems to be the last large work Ives undertook.

1927 ELEVEN SONGS, 1922–1927. A single bound volume of photostat mss. of songs composed after 1922, some of which were published by *New Music* in 34 SONGS or in 18 (19) SONGS. Not examined.

1928 UNIVERSE or UNIVERSAL SYMPHONY, 1911–1916, 1927–1928; a few notes were added from time to time, at long intervals, up to 1951. 'Preludes and sectional movement — uncomplete.' Only assorted pages of sketches seem to exist. Not intended to be completed by the composer himself nor by any other one man, because it represents aspects of life about which there is always more to be said.

S.R.C.

May 1954

Bibliography

Bellamann, Henry, 'Concord, Mass., 1840–1860, A Piano Sonata by Charles E. Ives,' *The Double Dealer*, Oct. 1921, 2:10, 166–9.

—— 'The Music of Charles Ives,' *Pro Musica*, Mar.–Apr. 1927, 5:1, 16–22.

—— 'Charles Ives, The Man and His Music,' *The Musical Quarterly*, Jan. 1933, 19:1, 45–8.

Carter, Elliott, 'The Case of Mr. Ives: Winter Nites,' *Modern Music*, Mar.–Apr. 1939, 16:3, 172–6.

—— 'Ives Today, His Vision and Challenge,' *Modern Music*, May–June 1944, 21:4, 199–202.

—— 'An American Destiny,' *Listen*, Nov. 1946.

Citkowitz, Israel, 'Experiment and Necessity,' *Modern Music*, Jan.–Feb. 1933, 10:2, 112.

Clough, Stephen B., *A Century of American Life Insurance, A History of The Mutual Life Insurance Company of New York, 1843–1943*, New York, Columbia University Press, 1946, 282.

'Composer Who Has Clung to His Own Way, The Life and Works of the New-found Charles Ives in Friendly Record,' *Boston Transcript*, 3 Feb. 1934.

Copland, Aaron, 'One Hundred and Fourteen Songs,' *Modern Music*, Jan.–Feb. 1934, 11:2, 59–64.

—— *Our New Music*, New York, Whittlesey House, 1941, 'The Ives Case,' 149–61.

Cowell, Henry, 'Four Little Known Modern Composers: Chavez, Ives, Slonimsky, Weiss,' *Aesthete*, Aug. 1928, 1:3, 1, 19–20.

—— 'Three Native Composers: Ives, Ruggles, Harris,' *The New Freeman*, 3 May 1930.

—— 'Charles E. Ives,' *Disques*, Nov. 1932, 3:9, 374–7.

—— 'Charles Ives,' *Modern Music*, Nov.–Dec. 1932, 10:1, 24–32.

—— ed., *American Composers on American Music*, Stanford University Press, 1933, 'Charles Ives,' by Henry Cowell, 128–45.

Darrell, R. D., comp., *Music Lovers' Guide*, New York, Feb. 1934, 'Living American Composers: Ives,' 173.

Downes, Olin, 'Music: Pro Musica Society,' *The New York Times*, 30 Jan. 1927.

—— 'A Lonely American Composer,' *The New York Times*, 29 Jan. 1939.

Furnas, T. Chambers, *The Mills of God, A Book of Essays and Poems*, Amesbury, Mass., The Whittier Press, 1937, 'Charles E. Ives, An Essay.'

Gilman, Lawrence, 'Music: A New Opera (Milhaud), a New Symphony (Ives) and a Debussy Fragment,' *The New York Herald Tribune*, 31 Jan. 1927.

—— 'A Masterpiece of American Music: The Concord Sonata,' *The New York Herald Tribune*, 21 Jan. 1939.

Harrison, Lou, 'On Quotation,' *Modern Music*, Summer 1946, 23:3, 166–9.

—— 'The Music of Charles Ives,' *Listen*, Nov. 1946.

Herrmann, Bernard, 'Charles Ives,' *Trend*, Sept.–Oct.–Nov. 1932, 1:3, 99–100.

—— 'Four Symphonies by Charles Ives,' *Modern Music*, May–June 1945, 22:4, 215–22.

'Insurance Man,' under Music, *Time Magazine*, 30 Jan. 1939.

'Ives & Myrick to Move in May,' *National Business Review*, Apr. 1926.

Ives, Charles, *The Amount to Carry—Measuring the Prospect*, pamphlet, New York, 1912; reprinted in *The Eastern Underwriter*, Sept. 1920, salesmanship edition.

Ives, Charles, *Essays Before a Sonata*, New York, The Knickerbocker Press, 1920.

—— 'Some Quarter-tone Impressions,' *Franco-American Music Society Quarterly Bulletin*, Mar. 1925.

—— 'Music and Its Future,' in Cowell, Henry, ed., *American Composers on American Music*, Stanford University Press, 1933, 191–8.

—— 'Children's Day at the Camp Meeting, A Program Note for the Fourth Violin Sonata,' *Modern Music*, Jan.–Feb. 1942, 19:2.

Lang, Paul Henry, 'Charles Ives, Hearing Things,' *The Saturday Review of Literature*, 1 June 1946.

Lederman, Minna, 'Some American Composers,' *Vogue*, 1 Feb. 1947.

Lieberson, Goddard, 'An American Innovator, Charles Ives,' *Musical America*, 10 Feb. 1939.

Mellers, W. H. 'Music in the Melting Pot: Charles Ives and the Music of the Americas, *Scrutiny*, Mar. 1939, 7:4, 391–401.

—— 'American Music, An English Perspective,' *The Kenyon Review*, Summer 1943, 365–6.

—— *Music and Society*, London, Dobson, 1946, 135–7.

Moor, Paul, 'On Horseback to Heaven,' *Harper's Magazine*, Sept. 1948, 65–73.

Myrick, Julian S. 'What the Business Owes to Charles E. Ives,' *The Eastern Underwriter*, 19 Sept. 1930, 18.

Rosenfeld, Paul, 'Charles E. Ives,' *The New Republic*, 20 July 1932, 262–4.

—— *Discoveries of a Music Critic*, New York, Harcourt, Brace & Co., 1936, 315–24.

—— 'Ives' Concord Sonata,' *Modern Music*, Jan.–Feb. 1939, 16:2, 109–12.

—— 'The Advent of American Music,' *The Kenyon Review*, Winter 1939, 1:1, 50–53.

—— 'The Advance of American Music,' *The Kenyon Review*, Spring 1939, 1:2, 187–8.

—— 'A Plea for Improvisation,' *Modern Music*, Nov.–Dec. 1941, 19:1, 15.

Rukeyser, Muriel, *A Turning Wind*, New York, Viking Press, 1939, 'Ives,' a poem.

Seeger, Charles, 'Grass Roots for American Composers,' *Modern Music*, Mar.–Apr. 1939, 16:3, 144.

—— 'Charles Ives and Carl Ruggles,' *The Magazine of Art,* July 1939.

Slonimsky, Nicolas, 'Charles Ives, Musical Rebel,' *Américas,* Sept. 1953, 7–8, 41–2.

Smith, W. Eugene, 'Charles Ives,' a photograph, *Life Magazine,* 31 Oct. 1949, 45.

Taubman, H., 'Posterity Catches Up with Charles Ives, An Interview,' *New York Times Magazine,* 23 Oct. 1949.

'Thoreau and Music,' *The Thoreau Society Bulletin,* Jan. 1947, No. 18; reprints *Thoreau,* No. 48, from *114 Songs,* by Charles Ives.

'To Continue Ives and Myrick Name,' *The Eastern Underwriter,* 23 Jan. 1943, 3.

Yates, Peter, 'Charles Ives,' *Arts and Architecture,* Sept. 1944, 20, 40.

Index

241